V. K. WELLINGTON KOO
AND CHINA'S
WARTIME DIPLOMACY

顧維鈞與中國戰時外交

by

William L. Tung

董　霖

Professor of International Law
and Far Eastern Studies
Queens College
The City University of New York

V. K. WELLINGTON KOO AND CHINA'S

WARTIME DIPLOMACY

DS
778
K59
T86
cp. 2

Published by

Center of Asian Studies
St. John's University
New York

Asia in the Modern World Series, No. 17

IN TRIBUTE TO

DR. V. K. WELLINGTON KOO

ON THE FELICITOUS OCCASION OF

THE NINETIETH ANNIVERSARY OF

HIS BIRTHDAY

A SELECTED LIST OF BOOKS BY WILLIAM L. TUNG

A. In English

China and Some Phases of International Law. London & New York: Oxford University Press, 1940.

Cases and Other Readings in International Law. Shanghai: Evans Books Co., 1940.

The Political Institutions of Modern China. The Hague: Martinus Nijhoff, 1964; 2d ed., 1968.

International Law in an Organizing World. New York: Thomas Y. Crowell Co., 1968.

International Organization under the United Nations System. New York: Thomas Y. Crowell Co., 1969.

China and the Foreign Powers: The Impact of and Reaction to Unequal Treaties. Dobbs Ferry, N.Y.: Oceana Publications, 1970.

Revolutionary China: A Personal Account, 1926-1945. New York: St. Martin's Press, 1973.

The Chinese in America. Dobbs Ferry, N.Y.: Oceana Publications, 1974.

V. K. Wellington Koo and China's Wartime Diplomacy. New York: St. John's University Press, 1977.

B. In Chinese

Imperialism in China. Shanghai: Kwaimin Press, 1930.

What Are the Three People's Principles? Shanghai: Kwaimin Press, 1930.

The Chinese Government. Shanghai: World Book Co., 1941, 2 vols.

The Chinese Constitutional Law. Chungking: Kuo-min T'u-shu Publications, 1943.

The Nationality Law of China. Chungking: Kuo-min T'u-shu Publications, 1943.

The Constitutional and Political Systems of Prewar China. Taipei: World Book Co., 1968.

Selected Essays on International Problems. Taipei: Hwa Kang Press, 1975.

Dr. Koo in his ambassador's uniform

Preface

A Chinese proverb says: "It is in the company of green leaves and blossoming peony flowers that the beauty is mutually reflected." It applies itself most fittingly to the relationship of Dr. V. (Vi) K. (Kyuin) Wellington Koo and Dr. William L. (Ling) Tung in the latter's present study of the former's achievements in China's war diplomacy.

Dr. Koo is not only a renowned diplomat-statesman in China of this century, but also a driving force in the world community. As Dr. Tung has already presented in this volume a detailed and systematic account of Dr. Koo's international and diplomatic life, it would be superfluous to add anything at all. Suffice it here to summarize his remarkable career in a very brief way.

Dr. Koo served the central government in Peking as Prime Minister, Minister of Foreign Affairs and other cabinet posts. As China's delegate to the Paris Peace Conference, 1919, he was, among his various distinguished contributions, a founder of the League of Nations along with Woodrow Wilson of the United States, Lloyd George of Great Britain and Georges Clemenceau of France. Also, he represented China at the Washington Conference, 1921-1922, and played an active role, resulting in the restoration of the Shantung rights to China.

Soon after the Mukden incident on September 18, 1931, the National Government in Nanking called on him to be Minister of Foreign Affairs and then Assessor representing China on the Lytton Commission of Inquiry.

During the Sino-Japanese conflicts, China was militarily too weak to confront Japan's aggression. Yet China was able to win political and diplomatic battles in the world assembly largely through the efforts and wisdom of her leading diplomats. Undoubtedly, Dr. Koo was one of them.

Under the Nationalist rule, Dr. Koo played an even more important role in China's diplomatic affairs. He was China's envoy to France and Great Britain. Soon after World War II, he was transferred from the Court of St. James to Washington as China's Ambassador to the United States. After he retired from his Washington post in 1956, he was elected in January 1957 concurrently by the Security Council and the General Assembly of the United Nations as judge of the International Court of Justice. For a decade, he served in that capacity (1957-1967) and also as Vice President (1964-1967) of this International Court at The Hague with great distinction. He has been not only a part of international history, but also a maker of it.

Dr. Koo's life and career have been embodied in the *Reminniscences of Wellington Koo* presented at Columbia University in May 1976 for future reproduction. It consists of eight volumes. It is no easy task even to provide a general sketch from this voluminous source material. Yet through his prolific pen and well-organized personal records and scholarship, Dr. Tung has been able to portray in this book an overall and yet very profound narrative of Dr. Koo's essential contributions both on the national and international levels.

Presently, Dr. Tung is Professor of International Law and Far Eastern Studies at Queens College of The City University of New York. As an eminent scholar and political scientist, he is the author of several significant books, notably *The Political Institutions of Modern China* (The Hague: Martinus Nijhoff,

1964), *International Law in An Organizing World* (New York: Thomas Y. Crowell, 1968), *International Organization under the United Nation's System* (New York: Thomas Y. Crowell, 1969), *China and the Foreign Powers* (New York: Oceana Publications, 1970) and *Revolutionary China: A Personal Account* (New York: St. Martin's Press, 1973).

Before he joined the academic world in the United States, he had a very close association with the public and diplomatic life of China. After World War II, he served as China's Ambassador to the Netherlands, Director of the Department of American Affairs and later Vice Minister of the Ministry of Foreign Affairs of the National Government. Because of his personal experience derived from these important posts, he is eminently qualified and competent to present this account of Dr. Koo's achievements, particularly during the war and post-war years.

St. John's University's Center of Asian Studies is most fortunate to be able to publish this admirable study by Dr. Tung as No. 17 in the *Asia in the Modern World Series.* As General Editor of this series, I am indebted to the author for his kind cooperation. In a special way I am most thankful to Mrs. Juliana Koo, wife of Dr. Koo, for her unfailing help in providing the photos and other generous assistance which are indispensable for bringing about this meaningful project.

January 1977

Paul K. T. Sih 薛 光 前
Vice President for International studies
and Education
and
Director, Center of Asian Studies
St. John's University, New York

Table of Contents

V. K. WELLINGTON KOO
AND
CHINA'S WARTIME DIPLOMACY[1]

CHAPTER ONE
Introduction

The devastating war Japan waged against China from 1937 to 1945 was actually a continuation of a series of prolonged

---

[1]This paper was prepared for delivery at the eighteenth annual conference of the American Association for Chinese Studies, held at St. Louis, Missouri, on November 5-6, 1976, under the general topic of wartime China. Its sources were partly drawn from *Reminiscences of Wellington Koo,* a massive autobiography of some 11,000 typed pages (a Chinese Oral History Project of the East Asian Institute of Columbia University, 8 vols.). On March 28, 1976, Dr. Koo was kind enough to make a copy available to this author for research on his diplomatic contributions to the twentieth-century China. In his letter of April 16, 1976, Dr. Koo wrote: "Referring to our conversation concerning your research on my life and career for future publication, I take pleasure in giving you permission to quote any part of my published and unpublished materials, including all the records of my interviews of my Oral Project at Columbia University." The original copy of his *Reminiscences* and related materials were presented to Columbia University on May 28, 1976. Acknowledgment should also be made of Mrs. Juliana Koo's gracious efforts to collect other materials for the use of the present research. The author is

hostilities between the two countries. [2] For the execution of their aggressive policies in the past decades, Japanese militarists and expansionists had resorted to various compulsory means,[3] including direct intervention, threat to use force, and outright invasion, a brief review of which is necessary to comprehend this tumultuous chapter of modern history. As a consequence of the first Sino-Japanese war (1894-1895), Japan acquired from China Taiwan (Formosa) and Penghu (The Pescadores), but failed to seize the Liaotung Peninsula in southern Manchuria because of the opposition of Russia, France, and Germany.[4] Notwithstanding the

---

grateful to Professors Paul K. T. Sih, Raymond L. Carol, and Leonard B. Allen, all of St. John's University, New York, Professor Irving L. Markovitz of Queens College of The City University of New York, and last but not least, my wife Portia, for reading the manuscript and making valuable suggestions.

[2]War has been outlawed by the General Treaty for the Renunciation of War of August 27, 1928 (generally known as the Kellogg-Briand Pact or Pact of Paris). Article 2 stipulated that "the settlement or solution of all disputes or conflicts of whatever nature or of whatever origin they may be, which may arise among them, shall never be sought except by pacific means." But the Treaty lacked any provision of sanctions against violators. For its text, see League of Nations, *Treaty Series,* Vol. 94, p. 57.

[3]For legal aspects of settling international disputes through compulsory means, see William L. Tung, "Settlement of Disputes through Non-amicable Means," in Albert Lepawsky and Harold D. Lasswell (eds.), *The Search for World Order* (New York: Appleton-Century-Crofts, 1971), pp. 97-119.

[4]Li Hung-chang, a renowned statesman and diplomat of the Ch'ing dynasty, was instrumental in persuading Russia to oppose the cession of Liaotung penisula to Japan. See *North-China Herald,* March 22, 1895.

three-power intervention, Japan had never given up her imperialistic schemes as fully manifested in the Twenty-One Demands in 1915,[5] as well as the forcible seizure of former German rights and interests in Shantung during World War I.[6]

It was most unfortunate that Japan deemed China's unity as her adversary. When the Nationalist Party (Kuomintang) launched its Northern Expedition to eliminate the remnant warlords,

---

[5] For the text of these Demands, see John V. A. MacMurray, *Treaties and Agreements with and Concerning China, 1894-1919* (New York: Oxford University Press, 1921, 2 vols.; hereafter cited as MacMurray, *Treaties,*) Vol. II, pp. 1231-1234. Dr. Koo returned to China from the United States, in 1912, to be an English secretary to President Yuan Shih-k'ai and Prime Minister T'ang Shao-i. Before taking up diplomatic missions abroad, he became secretary and later counselor of the Ministry of Foreign Affairs. When the notorious Demands were presented to Presdent Yuan, Lu Cheng-hsiang succeeded Sun Pao-chi as Foreign Minister to conduct negotiations with the Japanese Minister to China. Koo suggested that the support of foreign powers, particularly the United States and Great Britain, was absolutely necessary to counter the Japanese pressure. Thus during the course of negotiations, Koo, with the full approval of the President and the Foreign Minister, kept the American and British ministers (Dr. Paul Reinsch and Sir John Jordan respectively) informed. Through news purposely leaked out, China obtained the sympathy of the foreign press and the United States government, which had exerted some influence on Japan's subsequent decision to make certain concessions. See *Reminiscences of Wellington Koo*, Vol. II, pp. 74-90. For a brief account of the Twenty-One Demands and Sino-Japanese negotiations, see William L. Tung, *China and Foreign Powers: The Impact of and Reaction to Unequal Treaties* (Dobbs Ferry, N.Y.: Oceana Publications, 1970), pp. 154-159.

[6] Following her declaration of war against Germany, Japan conducted military operations in Chinese territorial waters and seized the German leasehold and a railway line in Shantung without the consent of the Chinse government. For China's protest, see MacMurray, *Treaties,* Vol. II, pp. 1154-1157.

Tokyo dispatched forces to Shantung and created the bloody
Tsinan incident in May 1928, for the purpose of preventing the
further advance of the revolutionary army under the command of
Generalissimo Chiang Kai-shek.[7] Failing to achieve their territorial
and economic ambitions in Manchuria, Japanese militarists
engineered the Mukden incident on September 18, 1931,[8] set up
the puppet state of Manchukuo in the following year, and
exhausted every means to detach North China,[9] culminating in the
full-scale war on July 7, 1937.[10] Compelled by circumstances,

---

[7]After protracted negotiations, an agreement for the settlement of
the incident was concluded between the two countries on May 28, 1929. For
the text of the agreement, see *Treaties and Agreements with and Concerning
China, 1919-1928* (Washington, D.C.: Carnegie Endowment for International
Peace, 1929; hereafter cited as Carnegie, *Treaties*), pp. 274-275.

[8]It has now been proved that the incident was purposely created
by Japan's Kwantung Army in Manchuria. See Chin-tung Liang, *The Sinister
Face of the Mukden Incident* (New York: St. John's University Press, 1969),
pp. 10-44.

[9]See *Papers Relating to the Foreign Relations of the United States*
(Washington, D.C.: Government Printing Office, 1861-; hereafter cited as *U.S.
For. Rel.*), 1935, Vol. III, pp. 342, 351, 390, 404, 420, 423-424, 426, 434,
448, 464, 468, 480.

[10]Japan preferred the term "hostilities" to that of "war" in order
to avoid the legal implications involving belligerent duties and neutral rights.
Actually, any armed conflict extending to a vast area is war in the material
sense, if not in the legal sense under the Charter of the United Nations. The
Japanese forces had traditionally resorted to sudden attack prior to a
declaration of war or even without it as in the present case, in contravention
of the Hague Convention on Opening of Hostilities of 1907. Texts of all
Hague Conventions with commentaries can be found in A.P. Higgins, *The
Hague Peace Conference and Other International Conferences Concerning the*

China was determined to meet the enemy's onslaught not only in the military field but also on the diplomatic front.

While this paper essentially deals with China's wartime diplomacy, occasional reexamination of certain prewar activities will help understand the sequence of events in proper perspective, particularly China's appeal to the Paris Peace Conference in 1919, the Washington Conference in 1921-1922, and the League of Nations in 1931 and the ensuing years. During the war, China had extensively engaged in bilateral and multilateral negotiations with major powers for strengthening her own position and restraining Japan's aggression. Chinese representatives had also actively participated in the establishment of international organizations of both political and non-political nature. Whereas China's foreign policies had been carried out by many eminent diplomats, the present research is chiefly concerned with the role played by V.K. Wellington Koo (generally known in China as Vi Kyuin Koo) because of his long service and unique contributions.

Ever since his completion of the Ph.D. degree in international law at Columbia University in 1912,[11] Koo had involved himself in

---

Laws and Usages of War (Cambridge, England: Cambridge University Press, 1909). For a judicial decision of the existence of war between China and Japan by the British Court of Appeal in 1939, see *Kawasaki Kisen Kabushiki Kaisha of Kobe v. Banthan Steamship Co.* (1939) 2 K.B. 54.

[11] In his *Reminiscences,* Koo gave a very interesting description of his childhood and education from 1888 to 1912. Born on January 29, 1888, he was the fourth child of Koo family in Kiating, a town twenty-four miles northeast of Shanghai. After his graduation from St. John's College in Shanghai, Koo came to the United States to study first at Cook Academy in the village of Montour Falls, N.Y. Beginning in 1905, he spent seven years in advanced research at Columbia University, where he also served on the

China's foreign affairs up to 1956 almost without interruption.[12] He was China's envoy to the United States (Minister, 1915-1920;

Students Board of Representatives and editor of the *Spectator*. As President of the Chinese Students' Club in New York and editor-in-chief of *The Chinese Students Monthly,* he acted as spokesman of the Chinese students invited by T'ang Shao-i to Washington, D.C. in 1908, when the latter was sent by the Imperial Court as a special envoy to see President Theodore Roosevelt. When Yuan Shih-k'ai succeeded Sun Yat-sen as President of the newly established Republic in 1912, T'ang became Yuan's Premier and was anxious to recruit young talents to help the country conduct foreign affairs. Recalling Koo's impressive personality and eloquence in the course of their previous conversation, T'ang recommended him to be an English secretary to the President and concurrently to the Premier's Office. See Vol. I, pp. 133-137.

[12]The Nationalist Party had a deep aversion to high-ranking officials in the Peking government, with the exception of those whose participation in the Peking hierarchy received its approval. Having held the portfolio of Premier and Foreign Minister, Koo was indistinguishably considered *persona non grata* by the National Government in Nanking. According to Koo, the situation was further complicated by the personal jealousy of a Nationalist official then in power. On July 11, 1928, the National Government issued a mandate for Koo's arrest. Chang Hsueh-liang (generally known as the Young Marshal), then political and military leader of Manchuria, deemed it unfair to treat Koo on the same level as many anti-Nationalist politicians in Peking, and volunteered to press for the cancellation of the mandate. After coming back from a European trip, Koo was appointed by the government in 1930 to be a member of the China National Exposition Commission. While he was in Shanghai for his mother's funeral, C. H. Wang, (Chung-hui Wang), then President of the Judicial *Yuan* of the National Government, went to urge him to go to Nanking. Wang told him that "the Generalissimo [Chiang Kai-shek] and other colleagues were asking me to understand that what happened in the mandate was something that never should have taken place, and therefore had it cancelled, and asked me not to misunderstand the purpose of the government." *Reminiscences of Wellington Koo,* Vol. III, p. 592. As a diplomat, Koo had the sole purpose of doing his best in the service of the government which represented China in international relations. Basically, he

Ambassador, 1946-1956),[13] Great Britain (Minister, 1921-1922; Ambassador, 1941-1946),[14] and France (Minister, 1932-1936; Ambassador, 1936-1941).[15] Koo was twice asked to be China's Ambassador to the Soviet Union, but, for personal and other reasons, he declined the offers.[16] Besides holding these major

---

has been an independent liberal without involving himself in party politics, even though he was later elected to the Central Committee of the Nationalist Party by the Sixth National Congress in 1945. At the time of national emergency after Japan's invasion of Manchuria, his talents were much needed. On November 28, 1931, he became Foreign Minister once more. Ever since, he had been at the service of the National Government until his retirement.

[13]It is interesting to note that Koo's first mission abroad was as Minister to Mexico. Before taking up the post, he was, however, transferred to the United States. This was a prearrangement by the Chinese government. Because of the importance of the Washington post, a senior diplomat was usually sent. Koo was then excessively young and had never been the head of a mission before. The Mexican assignment in August 1915 was solely designed to overcome Koo's lack of previous diplomatic experience. Having been officially notified of his second assignment, Koo presented his credentials to President Woodrow Wilson in December of the same year. For details, see *Reminiscences of Wellington Koo*, Vol. II, pp. 117-124. For a full account of Koo's first mission to the United States, see *ibid.*, Vol. II, pp. 119-256. His second mission lasted from 1946 to 1956, not to be discussed in this paper; records of his activities during that decade can be found in *ibid.*, Vols. VI-VII.

[14]Koo's first mission to London was comparatively brief (1921-1922), as described in *ibid.*, Vol. II. pp. 275-295. Vol. V is concerned with his second mission to London (1941-1946).

[15]Koo's long mission to Paris (1932-1941) was narrated in detail in Vol. IV.

[16]In June 1936, Koo was asked by the Chinese government to be Ambassador to Moscow after the resignation of W. W. Yen (Weiching William

diplomatic posts abroad, Koo was Minister of Foreign Affairs in 1922-1924 and again in 1926-1927 while concurrently serving as Prime Minister. Soon after Japan's invasion of Manchuria, he was called back by the National Government on November 28, 1931, to be Foreign Minister once more.[17]

For over four decades, Koo had represented China at all the major international conferences and organizations. Beginning in 1919, he attended the Paris Peace Conference as one of China's delegates and later, for all practical purposes, as head of the Chinese delegation.[18] A member of the committee to draft the Covenant of the League of Nations, Koo had taken an active part in the deliberations of its Assembly and Council meetings for a long period. He was Chinese delegate (1920-1922) and later chief delegate (1933-1936) to the Assembly, Chinese representative on the Council (1932-1934) and also President of its fourteenth and

------

Yen). Two years later, he was offered the Moscow post again. While appreciating the eagerness of the government to send its senior diplomat to the Soviet Union, he declind on both occasions. Koo considered "Paris a very good observation post, right in the heart of Western Europe." In his *Reminiscences,* Koo noted: "I had established good connections through which I could watch over the situation in Europe and try to get aid from different sources for China's cause." Vol. IV, pp. 415-417.

[17] For Koo's government service in Peking (1922-1928) and in Nanking (1931), see his *Reminiscences,* Vol. III. Reference may also be made to an unpublished doctoral dissertation by Pao-chin Chu, entitled *V.K. Wellington Koo: A Study of the Diplomat and Diplomacy of Warlord China, during His Early Career, 1919-1924* (University of Pennsylvania, 1970).

[18] A brief description of Koo's role at the Paris Peace Conference can be found in a booklet by Wunsz King, entitled *China at the Paris Peace Conference* (New York: St. John's University Press, 1961).

ninety-sixth sessions.[19]   Koo's connection with this first international organization also included his capacity as China's Assessor to the Lytton Commission of Inquiry, which was specially set up by the League in January 1932, to investigate the actual situation in Manchuria both before and after the Mukden incident. It was based on the report of the Lytton Commission that Japan was condemned as an aggressor.[20]

In addition to his activities at the League of Nations, Koo was appointed as a Chinese delegate to the Washington Conference in 1921-1922,[21] and successfully negotiated for the settlement of the Shantung problem with Japan. He represented China at the World Monetary and Economic Conference in London and the Geneva Conference for the Reduction and Limitation of Armaments in

---

[19]Koo's activities at the League of Nations can be found in his *Reminiscences*, Vol. IV.

[20]See League of Nations, *Official Journal*, Vol. 12 (1931), Pt. 2, pp. 2291, 2374-2375. The members of the Commission were General Frank R. McCoy (American), Lord Lytton (British), General Henri Claudel (French), Dr. Heinrich Schnee (German), and Count Aldrovandi (Italian), with Lord Lytton as Chairman. The Chinese and Japanese governments appointed one assessor for each side to assist the Commission, Wellington Koo and Isaburo Yoshida, respectively. See William L. Tung, *China and Some Phases of International Law* (New York: Oxford University Press, 1940, under the auspices of the Institute of Pacific Relations), pp. 164-168. China's official position can be found in *Memoranda Presented to the Lytton Commission by V.K. Wellington Koo, Assessor* (New York: Chinese Cultural Society, 1932, 3 vols.). See also *Reminiscences of Wellington Koo*, Vol. III, pp. 599-609.

[21]Wunsz King's *China at the Washington Conference* (New York: St. John's University Press, 1963) gave a brief review of the contributions made by the Chinese delegates.

1933. Subsequent to her appeal to the League of Nations, China sent Koo as chief delegate to the Brussels Conference, invoking the Nine-Power Treaty of 1922 for the preservation of China's territorial integrity and national sovereignty.[22] In carrying out many multilateral and bilateral negotiations with foreign governments during the war, Koo had played a pivotal role in strenghening China's diplomatic front.

For the planning of the postwar world, Koo was China's chief delegate to the Dumbarton Oaks Conference of the four major powers drafting proposals for a future international organization in 1944, acting chairman of the Chinese delegation to the San Francisco Conference for the establishment of the United Nations in 1945, and chairman of the Chinese delegation to the Preparatory Commission and the first session of the United Nations General Assembly at London and New York in 1945-1946. He also represented China on the War Crimes Commission at London in 1944-1946.

The scope of this paper excludes discussion of Koo's postwar activities as Chinese representative to the Far Eastern Commission on Japan (1946-1949),[23] Ambassador to the United States (1946-1956), as well as Judge and later Vice President of the

---

[22] For the text of the Treaty, see League of Nations, *Treaty Series,* No. 982 (1925), Vol. 38, p. 278; Carnegie, *Treaties,* pp. 89-93; *infra,* Appendix IV. For further discussion of the Treaty, see *infra,* Chapter 3.

[23] This Commission was to formulate policies, principles, and standards for Japan's fulfillment of the surrender terms. It was composed of representatives of China, Great Britain, the United States, the Soviet Union, France, Australia, Canada, New Zealand, the Netherlands, India, and the Philippines. Detailed information can be found in *Activities of the Far Eastern Commission* (Washington, D.C.: Government Printing Office, 1947).

INTRODUCTION

International Court of Justice (1956-1966).[24] The following pages cover only his important contributions in conjunction with China's wartime diplomacy.

---

[24]Unlike diplomatic missions, the International Court of Justice is an international agency, one of the main organs of the United Nations. It is composed of fifteen independent judges, elected regardless of their nationalities. For qualifications and elections of the judges and the competence of the Court, see William L. Tung, *International Organization under the United Nations System*, pp. 66-67, 92-95. For Koo's records of ten years in the International Court of Justice, see his *Reminiscences*, Vol. VIII.

CHAPTER TWO

Appeal to the League of Nations

The Sian incident in December 1936 was perhaps the turning point of China's domestic development and her relations with Japan.[25] The Nationalist-Communist reconciliation and the rapid consolidation of national unity soon after the incident were deemed by Japanese militarists as a direct threat to their numerous

---

[25]This incident occurred in Lint'ung near Sian on December 12, 1936, when Generalissimo Chiang Kai-shek was forciby detained by a *coup* led by two Nationalist generals, Chang Hsueh-liang and Yang Hu-cheng, over the issue of stopping domestic strife in order to resist Japan's aggression. They objected to Chiang's reasoning that the nation could not possibly carry out an effective war if internal riots were not first subdued. As a consequence of complicated negotiations. Chiang was released two weeks later and Nationalist-Communist reconciliation was worked out. For details, see Chiang Kai-shek and Madame Mei-ling (Sung) Chiang, *General Chiang Kai-shek: the Account of the Fortnight in Sian When the Fate of China Hung in Balance* (Garden City, N.Y.: Doubleday, Doran & Co., 1937); Chiang Chung-cheng (Kai-shek), *Soviet Russia in China* (New York: Farrar, Straus & Cudahy, 1957), pp. 72-79; *Mao Tse-tung: Selected Works* (New York: International Publishers, 1954-1962, 5 vols.), Vol. I, p. 255. For a brief analysis of the

plots in North China.[26] On July 7, 1937, they decided to strike a death blow at the Chinese forces stationed in the Tientsin-Peiping (Peking) area. The invading army first attacked Wanping, a Chinese district at the southern end of Loukou-Ch'iao (Marco Polo Bridge), on the pretense that China refused the entry of Japanese troops to search for a missing soldier. What appeared to be a local incident was predestined to develop into a full scale war. While resisting the aggressor on the battlefield, the National Government immediately instructed Chinese diplomats abroad to solicit the support of the major powers and the League of Nations, which was established for the maintenance of peace and order in the world.

Koo was then Chinese Ambassador to France. He hastened to discuss with the French Foreign Minister China's intention of applying Articles 10, 11, and 17 of the League Covenant, and also the possibility of joint action by France, Great Britain, and the United States. Article 10 of the League Covenant called for mutual guarantee of territorial integrity and political independence of member states. [27] Under Article 11, each member had the

---

incident, see William L. Tung, *The Political Institutions of Modern China* (The Hague: Martinus Nijhoff, 1964), pp. 163-165.

[26] The North China situation at that time was well described by Koo in his *Reminiscences*, Vol. IV, pp. 393-399. See also Shuhsi Hsu, *The North China Problem* (Shanghai: Kelly & Walsh, 1937), pp. 18-19.

[27] As shown in its text, Article 10 was particularly important to small or weak nations: "The Members of the League undertake to respect and preserve as against external aggression the territorial integrity and existing political independence of all Members of the League. In case of any such aggression or in case of any threat or danger of such aggression, the Council shall advise upon the means by which this obligation shall be fulfilled."

right to call upon the Council and the Assembly to discuss disputes.[28] This article was frequently the basis of action by the Council. While Article 16 applied to sanctions against an aggressor which was a member of the League,[29] Article 17 gave each League

---

[28] Art. 11 reads as follows:

"1. Any war or threat of war, whether immediately affecting any of the Members of the League or not, is hereby declared a matter of concern to the whole League, and the League shall take any action that may be deemed wise and effectual to safeguard the peace of nations. In case any such emergency should arise, the Secretary-General shall, on the request of any Member of the League, forthwith summon a meeting of the Council.

"2. It is also declared to be the friendly right of each Member of the League to bring to the attention of the Assembly or the Council any circumstance whatever affecting international relations which threatens to disturb international peace or the good understanding between nations upon which peace depends."

[29] Art. 16 was the backbone of collective security under the League of Nations system:

"1. Should any member of the League resort to war in disregard of its covenants under Articles 12, 13 or 15, it shall *ipso facto* be deemed to have committed an act of war against all other Members of the League, which hereby undertake immediately to subject it to the severance of all trade or financial relations, the prohibition of all intercourse between their nationals and the nationals of the covenant-breaking State, and the prevention of all financial, commercial or personal intercourse between the nationals of the covenant-breaking State and the nationals of any other State, whether a Member of the League or not.

"2. It shall be the duty of the Council in such case to recommend to the several Governments concerend what effective military, naval or air force the Members of the League shall severally contribute to the armed forces to be used to protect the convenants of the League.

"3. The members of the League agree, further, that they will mutually support one another in the financial and economic measures which are taken under this Article, in order to minimize the loss and inconvenience resulting from the above measures, and that they will mutually support one

member the same protection against a non-member state as that provided in article 16.[30]

It may be recalled that, on the basis of the Lytton Report, the Assembly decided, on December 9, 1932, to set up a Special Committee of Nineteen for the purpose of recommending some conciliatory measures for settling the Sino-Japanese dispute. Due to Japan's obstruction, the Special Committee failed to

---

another in resisting any special measures aimed at one of their number by the covenant-breaking State, and that they will take the necessary steps to afford passage through their territory to the forces of any of the Members of the League which are cooperating to protect the covenants of the League.

"4. Any member of the League which has violated any covenant of the League may be declared to be no longer a Member of the League by a vote of the Council concurred in by the Representatives of all the other Members of the League represented thereon."

[30]The following is the text of Art. 17:

"1. In the event of a dispute between a Member of the League and a State which is not a member of the League, or between States not members of the League, the State or States not members of the League shall be invited to accept the obligations of membership in the League for the purposes of such dispute, upon such conditions as the Council may deem just. If such invitation is accepted, the provisions of Articles 12 to 16 inclusive shall be applied with such modifications as may be deemed necessary by the Council.

"2. Upon such invitation being given, the Council shall immediately institute any enquiry into the circumstances of the dispute and recommend such action as may seem best and most effectual in the circumstances.

"3. If a State so invited shall refuse to accept the obligations of membership in the League for the purposes of such dispute, and shall resort to war against a Member of the League, the provisions of Article 16 shall be applicable as against the State taking such action.

"4. If both parties to the dispute when so invited refuse to accept the obligations of membership in the League for the purposes of such dispute, the Council may take such measures and make such recommendations as will prevent hostilities and will result in the settlement of the dispute."

accomplish its mission and submitted a draft report to the Assembly in accordance with Article 15 of the Covenant. On February 24, 1933, the Assembly adopted the report, consisting of four parts with proposals similar to the Lytton Report.[31] China voted for its adoption, but Japan replied by notifying of her intention to withdraw from the League. This was the reason why the Chinese government wanted to apply Article 17 instead of Article 16. Strictly speaking, the withdrawal would only take effect after two years' notice and Japan still had to fulfill all her international obligations, including those under the Covenant at the time of her notice of withdrawal.[32] Koo had intensified his consultation with the diplomats of the major powers, whose interests in China had been vitally affected by the war. [33] Regrettably, in the view of France and Great Britain, two pivotal members of the League of Nations, any League action would not be effective as shown in the past.

---

[31] League Doc. A (Extr) .22.1933.VII. See also League of Nations, *Official Journal, Special Supplement,* No. 1121, p. 13.

[32] See Art. 1 (3) of the League Covenant: "Any Member of the League may, after two years' notice of its intention so to do, withdraw from the League, provided that all its international obligations and all its obligations under this Covenant shall have been fulfilled at the time of its withdrawal."

[33] Since 1937, Japan had tried every means to monopolize China trade by adopting endless measures of restriction, prohibition and discrimination against foreign nationals. Because of many unwarrented acts committed by Japanese authorities in the occupied areas, France, Great Britain, and the United States made repeated protests. See V. K. Wellington Koo, *The Open Door Policy and World Peace* (Richard Cobden Lecture, published by Oxford University Press, London, 1939), pp. 18-22.

At that time, Finance Minister H.H. K'ung (K'ung Hsiang-hsi) was in London as China's special envoy and chief delegate to the coronation of King George VI. Koo went to London to discuss with K'ung the League attitude and European situation. Together with Quo Tai-chi, Chinese Ambassador to Great Britain, they jointly suggested to the government the importance of winning military cooperation of the Soviet Union as the first line of defense, backed by material support of France, Great Britain, and the United States for continued resistance. According to Ambassador T.F. Tsiang (Tsiang Ting-fu) who came from Moscow to join the London conversations, the Soviet Union would not be involved in a military entanglement against Japan nor would act alone diplomatically. Back in Paris, Koo tried to convince the Soviet ambassador to France of the importance of Soviet assistance to China in resisting their common enemy. Moscow's great reluctance in this regard was partly due to internal problems but primarily because of the Spanish situation and German hostility. It should be noted that the Sino-Soviet Non-aggression Agreement, concluded on August 21, 1937, did not have the same effect as a mutual defense treaty.

When the hope of joint action by the interested powers to stop Japan's aggression came to naught, the Chinese government decided to appeal to the League of Nations despite its weakened position after failure in settling the Manchurian incident, the Italo-Ethiopian war, and the Spanish situation. A League resolution condemning Japan's aggression would at least rally world public opinion to support China's cause, even if positive action might not be taken without the cooperation of Washington. It was important to consider which article or articles of the League Covenant should be applied. Any proposal for imposing sanctions against Japan would recognize a state of war between the two countries. The other states, particularly the United States, might enforce neutrality laws, which would be detrimental to China. In any event, China hoped very much to apply Article 17, even though the majority of League members would not take any measure of collective sanctions against Japan. France and Great Britain still held the position that the decision of appeal to the League was entirely up to China, but the result could be foreseen.

On August 30, 1937, Victor Hoo, Head of the Chinese Delegation's Bureau at Geneva, was instructed to hand the Secretary-General of the League of Nations a note, summarizing the Sino-Japanese situation as a continuation of Japan's aggression since 1931,[34] with the request that the Chinese views be communicated to the members of the Advisory Committee on the Far East. It may be recalled that this Committee was set up under the resolution of the League Assembly of February 24, 1933, to watch the development of the Sino-Japanese situation. It was composed of the original Special Committee of Nineteen plus Canada and the Netherlands. There was also an American observer on the Committee. While pursuing the instruction of the Chinese government to apply Articles 10, 11, and 17 of the League Covenant,[35] Koo took into consideration the unwillingness of

---

[34]The August 30th statement was followed by another one of September 12th, both of which can be found in C. Kuangson Young (ed.) *The Sino-Japanese Conflict and the League of Nations* (Geneva: The Press Bureau of the Chinese Delegation, 1937), pp. 108-113, 115-119.

[35]In his note to the Secretary-General of the League, Koo stated that "in the name of my Government, I hereby invoke the application of Articles 10, 11, and 17 of the Covenant and appeal to the Council to advise upon such means and take such actions as may be appropriate and necessary

Great Britain and France to impose sanctions against Japan and the importance of the United States cooperation with the League. Thus he adopted a flexible strategy so as to get the support of all interested parties.

After discussing China's appeal, the League Council, on September 16, charged the Advisory Committee on the Far East with examining the situation arising out of the Sino-Japanese conflict. On September 21, the day on which the Committee reconvened, the American government announced that it would attend on the same terms as in 1933. The Committee also invited China, Japan, Germany, and Australia to send delegates. As expected, Japan and Germany declined. After an intensive maneuvering at the Advisory Committee and its Sub-Committee, Koo, as head of the Chinese delegation, succeeded in having the Assembly adopt two reports on October 6, 1937: The first found Japan guilty of breaking her treaty obligatons; the second proposed what became the Brussels Conference in the following month,[36] and also recommended that the League members not only refrain from taking any action to weaken China's efforts to resist Japan but also consider extending individual aid to China.[37] The State Department declared its approval of the League action. According to Koo's evaluation, the outcome of the Assembly decision, though falling far short of China's expectations, was the

---

for the situation under the said articles." *Ibid.*, p. 120 The text of Arts. 10, 11, and 17 of the Covenant can be found in *supra*, notes 27, 28, 30.

[36] See *infra*, Chapter 3.

[37] For the text of the Report of the Far East Advisory Committee of October 5, 1937, see C. Kuangson Young, *op. cit.*, pp. 62-63

maximum result obtainable under the extremely difficult circumstances.[38]

Following the League resolution, Koo suggested to the Chinese government, on October 7, that it approach the powers concerned with definite proposals as to what kind of aid China would like them to supply. He also had discussions with his colleagues from Berlin, London, and Brussels, and with special envoys from China, including H. H. K'ung, Sun Fo, Li Yü-ying (also known as Li Shih-ts'eng), and Tsiang Pai-li, "trying to evaluate the world situation as a whole as bearing upon the Chinese situation, and trying to find some practical formula with a view to seeking and obtaining some effective aid from China's friends abroad."[39] Li, a senior member of the Nationalist Party, just came back from Moscow after his consultations with M. Litvinov (Soviet Commissar of Foreign Affairs), General Yang Chieh (new Chinese Ambassador succeeding T.F. Tsiang),[40] and American diplomats in Moscow. Tsiang, a foremost Chinese military strategist, was touring European countries, particularly Italy and Germany.

---

[38] Soon after the adoption of the Report, Koo wrote to T.F. Tsiang, Chinese Ambassador to Moscow, summarizing and evaluating the situation in details. See *Reminiscences of Wellington Koo,* Vol. IV, p. 671. In his *China and the League of Nations: The Sino-Japanese Controversy* (New York: St. John's University Press, 1965), Wunsz King gave a vivid description of Koo's diplomatic maneuvering leading to the adoption of the Report. See, particularly, pp. 83-87.

[39] *Reminiscences of Wellington Koo,* Vol. IV, Preliminary Draft, p. 31.

[40] Li was critical of T. F. Tsiang's lack of experience in dealing with the Soviet Authorities. See *ibid.,* p. 44.

K'ung as finance minister conducted negotiations for loans and credits in London and Paris and purchase of airplanes and munitions from the major powers in Europe. Sun Fo, President of the Legislative *Yuan,* devoted himself to seeking assistance from the Soviet Union. All the Chinese dignitaries had consulted with Koo on their different missions.

The year 1937 was most difficult for China, but her resistance to Japan was continuing. Disappointed with Generalissino Chiang's rejection of its peace terms, the Japanese government declared, on January 16, 1938, its decision to withdraw recognition from the National Government and openly sponsored the puppet regimes in China. Although diplomatic relations between the two countries were not formally severed, great pressures were put on Chinese consulates in Japan and Korea. To counteract Japan's military and political offensives, the Chinese government took all necessary steps, including a further appeal to the League of Nations.

At the one hundredth meeting of the League Council in Geneva in January-February, 1938, Koo kept himself extremely busy with exchanging views with the foreign ministers of France, Great Britain, the Soviet Union, and other powers. Upon his appeal, the Council adopted a resolution, on February 2, expressing its moral support to China and urging its members to consider aid to her. The resolution concluded by expressing hope for the feasibility of some further steps for a just settlement of the conflict in the Far East.[41] The lack of resolute measures by the League was disappointing, but this resolution was the most that could be expected in view of the preoccupation with the European situation and the unwillingness of the League members to impose

---

[41] For the text of the resolution, see *ibid.*, p. 67.

sanctions for fear of possible retaliations.

Meanwhile, China still considered that Article 17 of the Covenant should be applied by the League. After further negotiations with the diplomats of the major powers, Koo as Chinese chief delegate expounded China's legitimate request at the Assembly meeting on September 16, 1938. While sympathizing with the Chinese cause, the Scandinavian nations wanted the application of economic sanctions on the same voluntary basis as military sanctions. Concerned with the imminent invasion of Czechoslovakia by Germany, Great Britain and France pleaded with Koo to postpone the discussion of Article 17 of the Covenant. Even Secretary-General Joseph Avenol deemed that the meaning of Article 17 was not clear.[42] It is most unfortunate that the leaders of different governments at critical moments were often willing to sacrifice the essential principles of morality and international law for a temporary peace based upon injustice.

Legally speaking, collective measures, including military and economic sanctions, could be enforced by the League against an aggressor in accordance with Articles 16 and 17, even though the final decision of enforcing military sanctions was up to individual states, because the responsibility of the Council in this respect was limited to recommendations. On the other hand, economic sanctions were obligatory.[43] The League provision in this respect was different from that of the United Nations Charter.[44] "Under

---

[42] For details, see *ibid.*, pp. 228-251.

[43] See William L. Tung, *International Organization under the United Nations System,* pp. 161-162.

[44] Chapter VII of the United Nations Charter deals with

the League system, military sanctions were at the discretion of members, while economic sanctions against states violating the Covenant by resorting to war were automatically undertaken without waiting for the decision of the League Council",[45] practices to the contrary notwithstanding.

Disregarding the evasiveness of the Secretary-General of the League of Nations and the great reluctance of Great Britain and France to offend Japan in view of the European situation, Koo spoke to the Council on September 19, 1938, emphasizing "China's right to collective and individual aid" and reiterating "China's request to the Council for the immediate application of Article 17."[46] On the same day, the Council acted on the Chinese appeal by sending an invitation to the Japanese government to be represented at the League for the purpose of participation in the discussion of the dispute in accordance with Article 17, paragraph 1 of the Covenant.[47] Besides exchanging views with foreign diplomats attending the League Council, Koo was also busy in

----

enforcement measures and sanctions under different circumstances. The present writer is of the following opinion: "If there is a threat to or breach of the peace or an act of aggression, the Security Council may recommend action and call on members to apply economic sanctions and other measures short of war with a view to maintaining or restoring peace. In extreme cases, military action may be taken against an aggressor. Members of the United Nations have the obligation to accept and carry out decisions of the Security Council." *Ibid.*, p. 85.

[45] *ibid.*, p. 192

[46] *Reminiscences of Wellington Koo*, Vol. IV, Preliminary Draft, p. 262.

[47] For the text of Art. 17(1), see *supra*, note 30.

consultation with many Chinese statesmen visiting Geneva and his colleagues, including Hu Shih (newly appointed Ambassador to the United States succeeding C. T. Wang (Wang Cheng-ting), Ch'en Chieh (Ambassador to Germany), Quo Tai-chi (Ambassador to Great Britain), Tsien Tai (Ambassador to Belgium), and Wunsz King (Minister to the Netherlands). While all of them exerted efforts to work for League action,[48] the heaviest responsibility rested on the shoulders of the chief delegate.

As expected, Japan notified the League, on September 22, of her refusal to participate in the discussion. The League had to take action, because there was no reason for further delay. On September 30, the Council adopted a resolution that League members were entitled to take individually the measures provided for in Article 16.[49] But no effective measure was decided against Japan's air bombing of the civilian population.[50] Nor did the Council condemn Japan's use of poison gas; it merely advised the members to investigate cases brought to their notice and submit reports of their findings.[51]

---

[48] For Koo's comments, see *Reminiscences of Wellington Koo,* Vol. IV, Preliminary Draft, p. 272.

[49] For its text, see *supra,* note 29.

[50] A vague resolution against aerial bombardment of open towns and non-combatants was adopted by the Far East Advisory Committee on September 27, 1937, and by the Assembly on the following day. For its text, see C. Kauangson Young, *op. cit.,* p. 40.

[51] See *Reminiscences of Wellington Koo,* Vol. IV, Preliminary Draft, p. 275. The Chinese government had notified the League of Japan's use of poison gas as early as October 13, 1937. For the text of the Chinese communication, see C. Kuangson Young, *op. cit.,* pp. 87-89.

China's appeal to the League had reached the last stage without practical result. On October 24, Koo cabled a comprehensive report to Generalissimo Chiang, Premier H. H. K'ung, and Foreign Minister C. H. Wang, analyzing the international situation and its bearing upon China's policy *vis-a-vis* Japan. Among his recommendations, he urged continued negotiation for more Soviet aid and close cooperation with the United States with a view to applying economic sanctions, in collaboration with other powers, against Japan.[52] At that time, appeasement prevailed, as fully demonstrated at the Munich Conference. Nevertheless, concessions to an aggressor merely encouraged further aggression. With the eventual outbreak of World War II, the League of Nations itself virtually came to an end.

---

[52] See *Reminiscences of Wellington Koo,* Vol. IV, Preliminary Draft, pp. 279-284.

CHAPTER THREE
Invocation of the
Nine-Power Treaty

The Nine-Power Treaty was concluded at the Washington Conference (November 12, 1921 to February 6, 1922) on February 6, 1922.[53] While the Conference was convened essentially for the limitation of naval armament, China presented ten points for its consideration regarding her national sovereignty and territorial integrity.[54] Unlike their contemptuous indifference

---

[53] For the text of the Treaty, see League of Nations, *Treaty Series,* No. 982 (1925), Vol. 38, p. 278; Carnegie, *Treaties,* pp. 89-93; *infra,* Appendix IV.

[54] The text of the ten points can be found in *Conference on the Limitation of Armament, Washington, November 12, 1921 to February 6, 1922* (Washington, D.C.: Government Printing Office, 1922; hereafter cited as *Washington Conference, 1921-22*), pp. 866-868. These points were presented by Alfred Sze, who headed the Chinese delegation. Other delegates were V.K. Wellington Koo, C.H. Wang, and Chao-chu Wu. Representing the revolutionary government in Canton, Wu did not come to attend the Conference.

at the Paris Conference, the participants of the Western powers, particularly the United States, responded with sympathy and action at Washington. Elihu Root, who was entrusted to incorporate the Chinese proposals into a single resolution, submitted four clauses, which were duly adopted by the Conference on December 10, 1921. [55] The states with treaty rights and interests in China were Belgium, France, Great Britain, Italy, Japan, the Netherlands, Portugal, and the United States. Consequently, these powers and China signed the Treaty Regarding Principles and Policies to be Followed in Matters Concerning China, generally known as the Nine-Power Treaty. The signatories agreed to respect China's territorial and administrative integrity, and to prohibit any kind of discrimination in contravention of the Open Door Policy.[56]

As previously mentioned, the League of Nations, on October 6, 1937, resolved to adopt two reports submitted by the Advisory Committee on the Far East.[57] The second report provided that, whenever a situation should arise involving the application of the Nine-Power Treaty with respect to China's sovereignty and independence, as well as territorial and administrative integrity, there should be full and frank communication among the

---

[55] For the text of the Root Resolution, see *Washington Conference, 1921-22,* p. 900. For an analysis of the proposals contained in the Root Resolution, see W.W. Willoughby, *China at the Conference: A Report* (Baltimore: Johns Hopkins Press, 1922), pp. 43, 197.

[56] For the origin and effect of the Open Door Policy on China, see William L. Tung, *China and the Foreign Powers,* pp. 49-51, 54.

[57] For the text of the Assembly resolution and the two reports, see League Docs. A78.1937; A79.1937; A.80.1937.

signatories concerned. [58] In view of China's appeal to the League of Nations against Japan's aggression, the Assembly decided, by the same resolution of October 6, 1937, to invite those members of the League which were parties to the Nine-Power Treaty to initiate such consultation at the earliest practical moment. Letters of invitation were promptly sent to the powers concerned by the President of the League Assembly. Belgium was requested to act as the host of the Conference, which was to be held at Brussels on October 30, 1937.

In addition to the signatory states, the participants of the Brussels Conference also included five adhering powers with some but not substantial interests in the Far East, namely, Bolivia, Mexico, Denmark, Norway, and Sweden. Acting on behalf of the accepting powers, the Belgian government also invited Germany and the Soviet Union, both of which had direct interests in that region. Germnay declined the invitation on the ground that she signed but did not ratify the treaty; actually, as a political ally of Japan but with commercial interests in China, Germany did not want to offend either one of the disputing parties. The Soviet Union, not a party to the treaty but a member of the League of Nations, accepted the invitation. Japan declined to attend the Conference under the pretext that her controversy with China could only be resolved bilaterally.

What China hoped was to obtain a verdict of the Conference that Japan was an aggressor, wherby the powers concerned would extend material support to the victim in the form of military equipments, munitions, credits, and loans. According to China's expectation, such a verdict might also make it possible to have a

---

[58] League Doc. A80.1937.

show of force on the Manchurian border by the Soviet Union and possibly a naval demonstration in the Pacific by France, Great Britain, and the United States. At least, the participants of the Conference would refrain from giving financial and other material assistance to Japan. What the other powers had in mind was, however, to bring about a peaceful settlement between China and Japan through their efforts of mediation and conciliation.

Koo as China's chief delegate to the Conference had maintained close contacts with the Chinese government and its diplomatic representatives at various capitals, as well as the delegates of the participating powers. On October 28, he had a long conversation with Norman Davis, the American delegate, and his deputy Stanley Hornbeck,[59] when they stopped at Paris on their way to Brussels. In their view, the best way to settle the Sino-Japanese hostilities was through mediation by the powers concerned before any consideration of other positive steps against Japan. They reflected the opinion of President Franklin D. Roosevelt as expressed during his interview with C.T. Wang, Chinese Ambassador to Washington, and Hu Shih, then on a special mission in the United States. Davis and Hornbeck also suggested some strategy and procedures which China might adopt at the Conference. While promising to cable the Chinese government for instructions, Koo was by no means encouraged by their attitude.

---

[59] Dr. Hornbeck was in charge of the Far Eastern affairs in the State Department for a long period, and was eventually appointed United States Ambassador to the Netherlands in 1945. As my colleague at The Hague, we fully exchanged views of the American policy toward China both before and during the war. He explained that American public opinion at that time would not permit strong measures against Japan for fear of war.

The opening date of the Conference was postponed until November 3; it was attended by Eden of Great Britain, Delbos of France, Aldrovandi of Italy, Litvinov of the Soviet Union, Spaak of Belgium, and other important figures. Koo spoke in a conciliatory but firm manner. In preparing his speech, he had to take into account the opinions of various delegates whom he interviewed, at a time of a deteriorating military situation in China and rising demand of the Chinese people to continue the resistance for an eventual victory. The task was by no means easy. Koo exclaimed: "In the course of the years attending international conferences, it was rare that I felt strain of the work. But this time I was feeling very tired and was actually perspiring perhaps because of loss of sleep the night before."[60]

When the delegates were discussing the Far Eastern situation, there was a rumor that Germnay had already offered mediation but it was soon denied in Nanking, Tokyo, and Berlin. On November 7, the Conference sent a communication to the Japanese government, proposing that Japan accept mediation and also offering to appoint a small committee to exchange views with the Japanese representatives. Japan's reply on November 12 was a flat refusal on the ground that her action in China was a measure of self-defense and only concerned the two disputing parties.

The delegates at the Conference, much upset by Japan's curt and almost insolent refusal, deemed that there was no warrant in law for the use of armed force by any country for the purpose of interfering in the domestic affairs of another. On November 15, the Conference adopted a declaration, the last paragraph of which read: "The states represented at Brussels must consider what is to

---

[60] *Reminiscences of Wellington Koo*, Vol. IV, p. 815.

be their common attitude in a situation where one party to an international treaty maintains against the views of all the other parties that the action which it has taken does not come within the scope of the treaty which the other parties held to be operative in the circumstances."[61] Only the Italian delegate voted against it. Due to their limited material interests in the Far East and concerned with the obligations of imposing sanctions against Japan, the Scandinavian countries abstained. However, they were basically sympathetic to China. The purpose of the declaration, couched in moderate language, was intended to indicate tht the Conference was contemplating the adoption of a firm attitude toward Japan and undertaking consultations to line up the powers toward that end.

The Conference adjourned for a week, presumably to wait for the delegates to consult with their governments on the common attitude to be adopted and the next steps to be taken. But is was quite clear that the signatory powers abandoned any idea of adopting a hard attitude toward Japan. The British and French governments were busily occupied by the Spanish situation. By giving material support to the Franco government, Germany and Italy tried to detach Spain from French influence, thereby endangering France's communications with her African colonies. A hostile Spain would also threaten the British position in Gibraltar and the Mediterranean as a whole. Meanwhile, American public opinion and Congressional sentiment were not ready for supporting drastic steps against Japan.

The military situation in China was then developing from bad to worse. By the middle of November, Japanese forces took

---

[61] *Ibid.* Vol. IV, p. 837.

Taiyüan, the capital of Shansi province. The Shanghai defense line was broken, and the enemy headed for Hangchow and Nanking. On the other hand, China's stubborn resistance in the Shanghai area surprised the West and convinced the Powers that she was solidly united to fight for survival. The Conference resumed in the afternoon of November 22. A draft declaration prepared by the British and American delegates only stated vague principles without providing substantial proposals. In his speech, Koo pointed out that "solidarity in purpose should be followed by solidarity in action, and that by such an abortive ending as evidenced by the terms of the draft resolution the Conference would unwittingly augument the prevailing sense of general insecurity, rather than contribute to world order and stability."[62]

In spite of Koo's earnest plea, the Conference adjourned on November 24, 1937, after adopting a resolution reaffirming general principles and resorting to peaceful processes for the suspension of hostilities.[63] While offering a dim hope of its resumption, the Conference closed its doors for good. To express his complete disappointment with the participating powers at the Brussels Conference, Arnold Toynbee commented that "the spectacle of international anarchy moved them [delegates] not to try to put an end to it but simply to try to keep out of it." He compared their flight from Brussels "as ignominiously as Jos

---

[62]*Ibid.* pp. 926-927.

[63]Ambassador Tsien Tai, a Chinese delegate at the Brussels Conference, described its proceedings in a booklet, entitled *China and the Nine-Power Conference at Brussels in 1937* (New York: St. John's University Press, 1964). Appendix II contains the Report of the Conference of November 24, 1937. For its text, see *infra,* Appendix V.

Sedley had fled from the same city in June 1815 at the intimidating sound of the guns at Waterloo."[64]

It should be admitted that there was an inherent weakness of the Nine-Power Treaty, because it lacked a provision for enforcement measures. Actually, however, it would make no difference with or without any stipulation of sanctions, which would not be carried out anyway as in the experience of the League of Nations. In view of the infeasibility of taking effective action through collective means, the American and British delegates were willing to consider individually China's need outside the Conference.

---

[64] *Survey of International Affairs,* 1937, Vol. 1, pp. 52-53.

CHAPTER FOUR

Diplomatic Initiatives in Soliciting Foreign Assistance

While appealing to the League of Nations and the Nine-Power Conference at Brussels, China had simultaneously solicited individual support of the major powers. For that purpose, several government leaders were sent abroad as special envoys at different times: Sun Fo, President of the Legislative *Yuan*; H.H. K'ung, Finance Minister and later Prime Minister; T.V. Soong (Sung Tze-wen), Foreign Minister and later Prime Minister. Before the outbreak of World War II, Paris and Geneva were the best listening posts. Koo, as Ambassador to France and chief delegate to the League of Nations, was constantly consulted not only by the government but also by Chinese special envoys and diplomatic representatives stationed at other capitals.[65]

In Koo's opinion, a diplomat should always be concerned with

---

[65] See *Reminiscences of Wellington Koo,* Vol. IV, Preliminary Draft, pp. 358-364.

the problems in every quarter of the world. Thus his activities were not limited to Paris and Geneva; he frequently telephoned or wired his colleagues in London, Washington, Berlin, and Moscow, telling them what was the French attitude, what he was doing, and requesting them to take matters up with the respective governments of the countries where they were stationed.[66] He did likewise when he was accredited to the Court of St. James not long after the fall of Paris. At that time, Chinese ambassadors to Belgium, France, and the Netherlands were also in London with the exile governments.[67] The chief reason why this senior diplomat should take such initiatives might be attributed to his eagerness to serve his country with his vast experience in foreign affairs, unequalled by anyone in China or abroad. "I naturally would have expected the government to take the lead," Koo reminisced, "but knowing the situation in China and knowing that the personalities in China were often more immediately concerned with the situation at home, I felt it was my duty to do what I thought was the best thing to do, and then report back to the government and suggest what the next step should be."[68]

Of course, Koo had been very familiar with the Chinese

---

[66] For further comments on such matters, see *ibid.*, pp. 345-350.

[67] They were, respectively, Wunsz King, Tsien Tai, and the present writer, who became frequent guests of their senior colleague, Ambassador Koo, to exchange views among themselves and with visiting dignitaries from China and other countries, including Prime Minister Soong and Secretary of State Stettinius.

[68] *Reminiscences of Wellington Koo*, Vol. IV, Preliminary Draft, p. 348. See also *ibid.*, pp. 31, 279-285, 895-900.

situation in his capacity as Prime Minister, Foreign Minister, and in other cabinet posts of the central government in Peking. Soon after the Mukden incident on September 18, 1931, the National Government in Nanking called on him to be Foreign Minister and then as Assessor representing China on the Lytton Commission of Inquiry. When his mission to France was not busy during the period 1934-1936, he took a long home leave for personal observations of the political, economic, and social conditions in China. He was called back several times for consultations during and immediately after the war (October 1942 to March 1943, March-April 1945, and March-June 1946). This shows that, unlike many Chinese diplomats, Koo had kept close contacts with government leaders and their policies. Besides, the Nationalist hierarchy, including Generalissimo Chiang Kai-shek, had constantly asked his opinions on various problems in the world. On different missions during the war, Koo had also travelled over many parts of Europe and the United States and had important interviews with their leaders. Thus he was in a unique position to give counsel on diplomatic matters to his own government and his junior colleagues abroad.

Turning to Sino-Japanese relations, there were some indirect contacts for peaceful settlement during the early stage of the war. Despite official denials by the disputing parties, Japan made several attempts to induce China to accept mediation through Germany.[69] Beginning in November 1937, Oskar P. Trautmann,

---

[69] When Ch'en Kung-po, a close associate of Wang Ching-wei who later headed the puppet regime in Nanking, was in Rome in November 1937, both Mussolini and his Foreign Minister Ciano suggested mediation by Italy, but nothing was done. See *ibid.*, p. 7.

German Ambassador to China, secretly and repeatedly approached the Chinese authorities on peace terms, which in final form could be summarized as follows: (1) abandonment by China of the so-called anti-Japanese and anti-Manchukuo policies and cooperation of China in the execution of anti-Communist policy; (2) establishment of demilitarized zones and special regimes in Inner Mongolia, North China, and the occupied areas adjacent to Shanghai; (3) close economic cooperation with Japan and Manchukuo, which would be formally recognized by China; (4) indemnification to Japan. Since these conditions were totally unacceptable to China, any attempt to settle the Sino-Japanese dispute through mediation came to naught by the middle of January 1938.[70] China was more than ever determined to carry on the war, but foreign assistance was essential to effective resistance against the enemy.

In his reports to the Chinese government, Koo had frequently analyzed the interweaving relationships between the Far Eastern conflict and the European situation. Because of their rivalry with the Western democracies, Germany and Italy had made every conceivable move to direct Japan against Great Britain and France. They were even more anxious to see Soviet-Japanese relationships move from bad to worse. From the Chinese point of view, it would be most helpful to have Soviet military maneuvers along the Siberian-Manchurian border and British-French-American naval demonstrations in the Pacific. Toward that goal, Koo had approached the French government and the diplomats of these

---

[70]See "Reminiscences of President Chiang," *The Central Daily News* (an official newspaper of the Nationalist Party, issued in Taipei, Taiwan, in Chinese), July 6, 1976.

major powers in Paris and Geneva. But his efforts did not yield much results under the prevailing circumstances.

Although the Changkufang incident in the Summer of 1938 and the Nomonhan incident in May 1939 had created much tension along the Soviet-Manchurian border, Stalin did not want to wage a full-scale war against Japan unless the Western democracies would take collective action. Concerned with the aggressive designs of Germany and Italy, Great Britain and France were not in a position to adopt strong measures in the Far East without the initiative of the United States. Since President Roosevelt's "quarantine speech" received negative response from the American public,[71] Washington was not prepared to undertake joint action with the European democracies.

In view of the international situation prevailing at the time, China had to give up hope of Western military moves against Japan in the immediate future and to concentrate on efforts to win material assistance from the major powers. In this regard, the United States proved to be much more generous than other

---

[71] On October 5, 1937, President Franklin D. Roosevelt delivered this speech in Chicago, suggesting "quarantine" to prevent the spread of "the epidemic of world lawlessness." See Department of State, *Peace and War: United States Foreign Policy, 1931-1941*, Doc. 93, pp. 383-387. For an analysis of the impact of his speech, see W. L. Langer and S. E. Gleason, *The Challenge to Isolation, 1937-1940* (New York: Harper & Bros., 1952), p. 19. The American attitude of non-involvement had not been changed even after Japanese aviators sank the American gunboat *Panay* in the Yangtze River and killed two American crew without any provocation on December 12, 1937. A critical examination of the United States policy toward the Far East from the Japanese incursion into Manchuria and Jehol to the full-scale war can be found in Dorothy Borg, *The United States and the Far Eastern Crisis of 1933-1938* (Cambridge: Harvard University Press, 1964).

powers. During the period 1939-1941, American loans in exchange for tung oil, tin, tungsten, and other metals amounted to $120,000,000,[72] in addition to a credit of $500,000,000. In the successful negotiation of these loans, K. P. Chen (Chen Kuang-pu), President of the Shanghai Commercial and Savings Bank, made a great contribution. When Treasury Secretary Henry Morgenthau, Jr. visited Paris in July 1938, Koo had an intimate talk with him at the residence of American Ambassador William C. Bullitt on the United States financial assistance to China. Morgenthau recalled his previous experience with K. P. Chen in the purchase of Chinese silver, stating that "he found Mr. Chen a straight-forward and absolutely trustworthy businessman, in whom he has complete confidence."[73] He answered Koo that some positive arrangement could be made if the Chinese government would send Chen to Washington at the beginning of September. Upon Koo's information, the Chinese government persuaded Chen to undertake the mission, which was amply rewarded.[74]

---

[72] This amount represented the following loans: tung oil loan (1939), $25,000,000; tin loan (1940), $20,000,000; tungsten loan (1940), $250.000,000; metal loan (1941), $50,000,000. See *China Handbook, 1937-1945* (New York: The Macmillan Co., 1947, compiled by the Chinese Ministry of Information), p. 150.

[73] *Reminiscences of Wellington Koo,* Vol. IV, Preliminary Draft, p. 188. Chen once told Morgenthau that "he was no diplomat nor statesman, and never wished to enter politics on the ground that politicians died earlier and he wished to live to a ripe old age." *Loc. cit.* Chen had indeed lived a long life. He died in July 1976, at the age of ninety-six.

[74] See "Reminiscences of President Chiang," *The Central Daily News,* August 11, 1976. In this connection, it may help understand the

This proved that diplomacy had a great deal to do with personal image and mutual confidence. Pleased with the large amount of the American loan, Finance Minister H.H. K'ung sent a special cable to Koo to express the deep gratitude of the Chinese

---

process of Chen's loan negotiations by quoting a part of a letter addressed to the present writer by C. Tsang (Tsang Chih), President of the New World Research Corporation of New York, who was a close associate of Chen and former secretary-general of the Universal Trading Corporation of New York, founded by Chen to carry out Sino-American commercial transactions for the implementation of the loan agreements:

"I remembered one morning, Mr. Chen told us that Dr. K'ung had invited him to his house and informed him that the government and the Generalissimo must ask him to go to USA again, this time to seek financial help from the US government. He remonstrated with Dr. K'ung that the responsibility was too big for a private individual like him and that he certainly would not dare to play with the fate of China. But Dr. K'ung told him bluntly that it was not the Chinese government who wanted to send him but his friend Morgenthau who wanted him to go there for the Chinese government. He showed him the cables received from Dr. Koo. Obviously, he could not refuse, but what form of assistance could he ask from the US government? At that time, probably not even Secretary Morgenthau had any idea as to how assistance could be arranged nor the Chinese government knew what arrangement could be made under the prevailing circumstances except to send Mr. Chen and do whatever the US government wanted. It was Mr. Chen's idea that any proposal submitted to the US government must be judged from the lender's side, not from the borrower's side, so that it could be acceptable. Being a banker, he must do what was practical and must do it successfully. On the basis of this principle, he hit upon the brilliant idea of arranging a commercial loan with wood oil as security. It was commercial in nature having nothing to do with the law of neutrality, and Congress could not make any issue of it, yet it had a great moral value in that the establishment of this loan clearly indicated that the US government was on our side and the balance of power in the world situation was being tipped in our favor. It had also the practical value of using the proceeds of the loan to purchase trucks and many other items of military supplies which were urgently needed." (C. Tsang's letter to William L. Tung, dated September 1,

government for his efforts in assisting the negotiation.[75] On June 2, 1942, the Sino-American Lend-Lease Agreement was signed, laying down the principle of mutual aid in the prosecution of the war. Thenceforth, American aid was extended from financial to military assistance, even though it was limited by Europe-first strategy and transportation difficulties.

British export credit loans to China from 1939 to 1941 totalled £8,047,000.[76] Following the American grant of government credit of $500,000,000, the British government announced a credit of £50,000,000 to China chiefly for the purchase of trucks, but the frustrated negotiation for its implementation resulted in some unnecessary misunderstandings. Koo exerted maximum efforts to persuade the French government to extend some material assistance to China, including the purchase of war materials and munitions as well as transit facilities through Indochina. Due to its own rearmament porgram in the face of the German threat, however, only a small quantity could be diverted to China.

Koo had also maintained frequent contacts with Foreign Minister Maxim Litvinov, when both headed Soviet and Chinese

1976.) The wood or tung oil loan was soon followed by the tin loan and other transactions, which proved to be invaluable to China.

[75] K'ung's cable dated December 26, 1938, when the negotiation for the tung oil loan was practically completed. See *Reminiscences of Wellington Koo*, Vol. IV, Preliminary Draft, p. 418.

[76] This amount represented the following loans: first export credit loan (1939), £188,000; second export credit loan (1939), £2,859,000; third export credit loan (1941), £5,000,000. See *China Handbook*, 1937-1945, p. 164.

delegations to the League of Nations meetings at Geneva. Following the conclusion of the Sino-Soviet Non-Aggression Treaty of August 21, 1937, [77]the Soviet government granted credit loans to China three times, totaling $250,000,000.[78] Sun Fo, President of the Legislative *Yuan,* made several trips to Moscow, negotiating for Soviet financial and military assistance to China.[79] But the signing of the Soviet-Japanese Treaty of Neutrality and Friendship on April 13, 1941 stopped further cooperation between Moscow and Chungking.

---

[77]For the text of the Treaty, see Chinese Republic, *Treaties,* pp. 486-487; Yin-ching Chen (ed.), *Treaties and Agreements between the Republic of China and Other Powers, 1929-1954* (Washington, D.C.: Sino-American Publishing Service, 1957; hereafter cited as Chen, *Treaties*), pp. 113-114. China had originally hoped to conclude a treaty of alliance with the Soviet Union. This task was confidentially undertaken by Chen Li-fu, who together with his elder borther Kuo-fu had long been in charge of the organization of the Nationalist Party. On his way to Moscow, he waited in Berlin for further instructions. Stalin's final decision not to offend Japan rendered Chen's mission unfulfilled. This information was conveyed by Chen to the present writer in person. See William L. Tung, *Revolutionary China: A Personal Account, 1926-1945* (New York: St. Martin's Press, 1973), p. 240. For Koo's suggestion to conclude a general pact of non-aggression and mutual assistance for the Pacific and Far Eastern regions and other related proposals, see *Reminiscences of Wellington Koo,* Vol. IV, pp. 458-463, 491-522.

[78]This amount represented the following: two credit loans in 1938, $50,000,000 each; third credit loan in 1939, $150,000,000. See *China Handbook, 1937-1945,* p. 167. A Sino-Soviet Commercial Treaty was signed on June 16, 1939; its text can be found in Chinese Republic, *Treaties,* pp. 488-499.

[79]In his trips to Moscow, Sun Fo usually stopped at Paris and exchanged views with Koo. See *Reminiscences of Wellington Koo,* Vol. IV, Preliminary Draft, pp. 168, 703.

The shipping of war materials to China had become a most difficult problem. Notwithstanding his ceaseless efforts to seek its solution with the French government, Koo had been confronted with almost insurmountable obstructions. It should be noted that the northwest road from the Soviet Union to Sinkiang was not suitable for large shipments. Due to Japanese pressure, the British government announced, on July 17, 1940, the closing of the Burma Road for three months. [80] As Chinese Ambassador to France at that time, Koo had spent much time negotiating with the French authorities for transit facilities through Indochina, but their cooperation in this respect was rather limited on the ground of French military weakness in the Far East and lack of a commitment of mutual assistance from Great Britain and the United States. [81]

Legally speaking, Great Britain and France had both the right and obligation to aid China on the basis of the League of Nations resolution in February 1933, which declared that Japan committed an aggression against China. Under the Covenant, any aggression against a member of the League was considered an aggression against all other members. [82] In the case of Indochina,

---

[80] See "Reminiscences of President Chiang," *The Central Daily News*, August 16, 23, 1976.

[81] On this subject, Koo made repeated representations to the French government, particularly to Ministers of Foreign Affairs and of Colonies. In his interview with Foreign Minister Georges Bonnet on April 21, 1938, Koo protested in very strong terms against restrictions of transit facilities through Indochina. For details, See *Reminiscences of Wellington Koo*, Vol. IV, Preliminary Draft, p. 110.

[82] See Art. 16(1) of the League Covenant, the text of which can be found in *supra*, note 29.

China's right of transit was stipulated in the Sino-French Convention of May 16, 1930, which came into effect on July 22, 1935.[83] While French Foreign Minister Georges Bonnet was too cautious, other leaders, including Premier Edouard Daladier, were more sympathetic to China's requests by granting the passage of war materials and planes through Indochina. However, by late June 1940, soon after the French surrender to Germany, transit facilities through Indochina practically stopped.[84]

---

[83] For the text of the Convention, see Chen, *Treaties*, pp. 52-59. See also *Reminiscences of Wellington Koo*, Vol. IV, pp. 688-693.

[84] For French-Japanese relations, particularly concerning Indochina after French surrender to Germany, see *ibid.*, Preliminary Draft, pp. 1208-1209, 1222, 1250, 1319-1320.

CHAPTER FIVE

Elevation of China as a Major Power

The courage and tenacity of the Chinese forces to carry out the war of resistance against Japan's invasion had quite impressed President Roosevelt, who was determined to raise China's status as one of the great powers. What Roosevelt had in mind was that, after the defeat of Japan, China would become the major stabilizing factor in the Far East during the postwar period. Thus he moved to invite her to join the Moscow Declaration on General Security of October 30, 1943.[85] It was true that China's participation was solely due to Roosevelt's insistence over the initial reluctance and even objections by Stalin and Churchill.[86]

---

[85] For its text, see *Yearbook of the United Nations,* 1946-47 (New York: Department of Public Information, United Nations, 1947), p. 3.

[86] On this delicate issue, Koo noted in his *Reminiscences* the following: "Our position as one of the four great powers had been achieved at President Roosevelt's insistence through Cordell Hull at Moscow when we

Signed by the representatives of Great Britain, the Soviet Union, China, and the United States, this four-power declaration agreed on the necessity of establishing a general international organization at the earliest practical date.[87]

The most important wartime conference for China was held at Cairo, on November 22-26, 1943, attended by President Roosevelt, Prime Minister Churchill, and Generalissimo Chiang Kai-shek. Although a large-scale amphibious campaign against Japan as previously agreed upon by the Allied powers was abandoned after the Teheran Conference, they proclaimed on behalf of their respective governments on December 1, 1943:

> "It is their purpose that Japan shall be stripped of all the islands in the Pacific which she has seized or occupied since the beginning of the first World War in 1914, and that all the territories Japan has stolen from the Chinese, such as Manchuria, Formosa, and the Pescadores, shall be restored to the Republic of China. Japan will also be expelled from all other territories which she has taken by violence and greed. The aforesaid three great powers, mindful of the

---

were brought in at the last minute. Even then England had opposed us. But of course Churchill did not want to oppose Roosevelt too much when Roosevelt took a firm stand." Vol. V, p. 818. However, Cordell Hull once told Koo that "it had been Stalin who first had put up strong opposition to China's signing." In Koo's view, "it is possible that both Churchill and Stalin had opposed." *Ibid.*, p. 678.

[87]The representatives were Anthony Eden, Vyacheslav S. Molotov, Foo Ping-sheung (Chinese Ambassador to Moscow), and Cordell Hull, respectively. According to Art. 4 of the Moscow Declaration, this general international organization should be "based on the principle of sovereign equality of all peace-loving states, and open to membership by all such states, large and small, for the maintenance of international peace and security."

enslavement of the people of Korea, are determined that in
due course Korea shall become free and independent."[88]

At this juncture, perhaps mention should be made of a
conversation between Chiang and Roosevelt about Port Arthur, a
strategic seaport in Manchuria adjacent to the commercial port
Dairen. The lease and joint administration of these two ports were
later demanded by Stalin at Yalta as one of the conditions for
Soviet entrance into the war against Japan. According to Koo,
Generalissimo Chiang told President Roosevelt at Cairo that Port
Arthur could be utilized jointly by China and the United States as
a naval base, but this was only a verbal offer and nothing came out
of it.[89]

The Cairo commitments as stated above were reaffirmed by
the Potsdam Proclamation Defining Terms for Japanese Surrender
of July 26, 1945, which read, in part, as follows: "The terms of
the Cairo Declaration shall be carried out and Japanese sovereignty
shall be limited to the islands of Honshu, Hokkaido, Kyushu,
Shikoku and such minor islands as we determine."[90] The Allied

---

[88] Chen, *Treaties*, p. 174. The full text of the Cairo Declaration can
be found in *ibid.*, pp. 173-174.

[89] This significant event was related to Koo by Hsiung Shih-hui, one
of Chiang's most trusted generals. He was once head of the Chinese military
mission to the United States. It was confirmed by C. H. Wang in a
conversation with Koo in Chungking, on March 19, 1945. Wang was then
Secretary-General of the Supreme National Defense Council. A man of few
words with a reputation of discretion and integrity, Wang accompanied
Chiang to Cairo as his high adviser. For details, see *Reminiscences of
Wellington Koo,* Vol. V, p. 768.

[90] For the text of the Proclamation, see *Chen,* Treaties, pp. 216-217.

Powers had fully carried out the provisions of the Cairo Declaration. There is not the slightest doubt that Taiwan (Formosa) and Penghu (The Pescadores) belong to China despite illogical statements from certain official quarters in later years. It is a pity that, in world politics, overemphasis of national interests and consideration of international expediency often overshadowed the legal position of a problem.[91]

Perhaps one of China's most important accomplishments which had considerably raised her status in the world was the termination of extraterritoriality and other related rights of the interested powers, particularly Great Britain and the United States. It had been the cherished hope of the Chinese government and people to abolish all the unequal treaties imposed on China by the Western powers and Japan.[92] As a delegate to the Paris Peace Conference in 1919 and the Washington Conference in 1921-1922, Koo had presented China's case most eloquently.[93] The *desiderata* presented to the Paris Conference consisted of such questions for

----

[91] Concerned with the possible loss of these islands to the Chinese Communists, President Truman raised the question of their status after the outbreak of the Korean War on June 27, 1950. Another statement made by a State Department spokesman, on April 28, 1971, also invited much criticism. For details of the present writer's comments, see Roslyn Kaplan and Mathilde Genovese (eds.), *William L. Tung's Commentaries on World Affairs* (New York: Queens College, CUNY, 1974), pp. 37-38

[92] For details of foreign intrusions on China's national sovereignty and territorial integrity, see William L. Tung, *China and the Foreign Powers*, pp. 69-144.

[93] Many of Koo's early speeches are contained in Wunsz King, *V.K. Wellington Koo's Foreign Policy: Some Selected Documents* (Shanghai: Kelly & Walsh, 1931).

readjustment as spheres of influence, the presence of foreign armed forces and police, foreign post offices and wireless stations, leased territories, foreign concessions and settlements, extraterritoriality, and uniform tariff. But Premier Georges Clemenceau of France on behalf of the Council of Four advised the Chinese delegation that China's proposals did not "fall within the competence of the Paris Conference."[94]

The Washington Conference took a receptive attitude toward the "Ten Points" presented by China,[95] but the Western powers were most reluctant to relinquish the uniform tariff and extraterritoriality in China.[96] The Chinese government continued to negotiate with the powers concerned on the two questions. Led by the Sino-American Treaty of July 25, 1928, restoring "the

---

[94] See *U. S. For. Rel., Paris Peace Conference* (13 vols.), Vol. 5, p. 621. For the text of Chinese proposals, see "Questions for Readjustment," submitted by China to the Paris Peace Conference of 1919, in *Chinese Social and Political Science Review,* Vol. 5a (1919-1920), pp. 115-170. At Paris, China was most concerned with the return of former German rights and interests in Shantung. The arbitrary decision of the Council of Four to transfer them to Japan resulted in China's refusal to sign the Treaty of Versailles. For details, see *Reminiscences of Wellington Koo,* Vol. III, pp. 217-243.

[95] For the text of the Ten Points, see *Washington Conference, 1921-22,* pp. 866-868.

[96] For a summary and evaluation of the Washington Conference concerning China, see William L. Tung, *China and the Foreign Powers,* pp. 185-218. Besides Koo, there were two more Chinese delegates at the Washington Conference: Alfred Sze (head of the delegation) and C.H. Wang. Koo took charge of the following questions: the leased territories, the sphere of influence, the customs tariff, the Shantung question, and the abrogation or the revision of unequal treaties. Sze chose the question of the withdrawal of

principle of complete national tariff autonomy to China,"[97] other countries concluded similar treaties in the ensuing years. But the discussion of extraterritorial jurisdiction was suspended after the outbreak of the Sino-Japanese war.[98]

In May 1941, the State Department expressed its willingness to resume discussion with the Chinese government on extraterritoriality after the restoration of peace. When China became an ally of the Western Democracies after Pearl Harbor, the United States and Great Britain decided to comply with China's wishes in this respect by declaring their intention for its immediate relinquishment. It did not take long to complete the Sino-American negotiation toward that end. But the negotiation for the Sino-British Treaty met some obstacles, particularly because of China's insistence on including in the treaty the return of the leased territory of Kowloon,[99] adjacent to Hongkong. In

---

armed forces and the relinquishment or the abolition of foreign post offices. Wang volunteered to take charge of the questions of the return of foreign concessions, the termination of extraterritoriality, and the cancellation of the Twenty-One Demands imposed on China by Japan in 1915. See *Reminiscences of Wellington* Koo, Vol. III, pp. 271-272. It should be noted that the Shantung question was settled collaterally with the Washington Conference. See *ibid.*, pp. 279-295.

[97] For the text of the Treaty, see Carnegie, *Treaties,* pp. 230-231; Chinese Republic, *Treaties,* pp. 648-649.

[98] For a summary of China's efforts to abolish unequal treaties from 1927 to 1937, see William L. Tung, *China and the Foreign Powers,* pp. 249-257, 275-283; also comments on the subject by the same author in Paul K. T. Sih (ed.) *The Strenuous Decade: China's Nation-Building Efforts, 1927-1937* (New York: St. John's University Press, 1970), pp. 29-31.

[99] The leased territory of Kowloon was based on the Sino-British

the view of the British government, the Kowloon question had no bearing on the contemplated treaty For a time, the negotiation almost reached impasse.

Koo was then Chinese Ambassador to Great Britain and returned to Chungking for consultations. As an experienced diplomat well familiar with the attitude of British official and unofficial circles, he counselled the government to conclude the treaty on the relinquishment of extraterritoriality but reserve the right of later negotiation on the Kowloon question. Discussions among Generalissimo Chiang and other party and government leaders resulted in their concurrence with Koo's views.[100] Consequently, the Chinese government simultaneously signed, on January 11, 1943, the Treaty for the Relinquishment of Extraterritorial Rights in China and the Regulation of Related Matters with the United States at Washington and with Great Britain at Chungking.[101]

Convention for the Extension of Hongkong, signed on June 9, 1898. The duration of its lease was ninety-nine years. For its text, see MacMurray, *Treaties*, Vol. I, pp. 130-131. It is interesting to note that, notwithstanding the delay of restoring Kowloon to China, Great Britain took the lead to negotiate for the return of the leased territory Weihaiwei at the Washington Conference (1921-1922). Koo as Foreign Minister had prepared a draft agreement for that purpose, but the change of the government late in 1924 postponed its conclusion until 1930. See *Reminiscences of Wellington Koo*, Vol. III, p. 491.

[100] In his *Reminiscences*, Koo described vividly the frustrated negotiations with the British government and the exchange of views among the Chinese leaders themselves. See Vol. V, pp. 175, 271-300. See also "Reminiscences of President Chiang," *The Central Daily News*, October 6, 1976.

[101] For the text of these two treaties, see Chinese Republic, *Treaties*,

With the precedents set by the United States and Great Britain, other countries soon followed suit.[102] Among the major powers, France was in a difficult position because of the practical existence of two governments as a consequence of German occupation. Thus the Sino-French treaty for the relinquishment of extraterritorility was not signed until February 8, 1946.[103] The Soviet Union relinquished extraterritoriality in China soon after the Revolution. Germany, Austria, Italy, and Japan lost their treaty rights as a consequence of the war in accordance with the general rules of international law.[104] Thus China finally liberated herself

---

pp. 659-669, 589-599, respectively. The two treaties were originally scheduled for signature on January 1, 1943. This news was prematurely reported by the Chungking edition of *The Central Daily News,* which was under the supervision of the Ministry of Information. Chiang was infuriated by the leak and ordered the punishment of the editorial staff responsible for it. The present writer was then concurrently Secretary-General of the Ministry, and naturally felt very much embarrased by the incident. The Chinese government had previously given Sir Horace Seymour, British Ambassador to China, the impression that the failure of settling the Kowloon problem might result in the breakdown of the negotiation. Thus the premature publicity of the signing date by a party paper was deemed harmful to China's bargaining power. The eventual postponement of the signing date was, however, not due to the leak, but because of Washington's desire to have more time checking the translation of the text. See *Reminiscences of Wellington Koo,* Vol. V. pp. 279-287; William L. Tung, *Revolutionary China: A Personal Account, 1926-1945,* pp. 244-245.

[102] See William L. Tung, *China and the Foreign Powers,* p. 272. For a brief account of China's diplomatic relations with other countries, see *China Handbook,* 1937-1945, pp. 165-167, 174-186.

[103] For its text, see Chinese Republic, *Treaties,* pp. 152-160; Chen, *Treaties,* pp. 259-265.

[104] While there are no definite rules governing the termination of

from the century-old bondage of unequal treaties.

---

treaties among belligerents as a consequence of war, it is the general practice that "executory treaties relating to alliance, commerce, navigation, and treaties exclusively for peacetime purposes are terminated." On the other hand, "executed or dispositive treaties for cession, boundaries, and others of permanent nature are merely suspended." Likewise are "multilateral instruments, especially law-making treaties." William L. Tung, *International Law in an Organizing World*, p. 363.

CHAPTER SIX
Interallied Friction

Whereas China's friendly relations with the United States were further advanced by the American repeal of all the Chinese exclusion acts on December 17, 1943,[105] there was some friction between the two countries. Generalissimo Chiang felt that the American attitude toward China was too dictatorial. Because of the Europe-first strategy, the amount of aid to China could not possibly compare with that to Great Britain and the Soviet Union. On the other hand, American leaders were disappointed with China's domestic situation and her lack of maximum efforts in executing the war. After his return from a Far Eastern trip, Vice President Henry A. Wallace submitted an unfavorable report to President Roosevelt, pointing out that the Chinese morale was low

---

[105] For the text of An Act to Repeal the Chinese Exclusion Acts, to Establish Quotas, and for Other Purposes of December 17, 1943, see William L. Tung, *The Chinese in America* (Dobbs Ferry, N.Y.: Oceana Publications, 1974), pp. 79-80. For the discriminatory treatment of the Chinese in the United States prior to the 1943 Act, see *ibid.*, pp. 6-32.

and that the government was liable to topple.[106] Madame Chiang's sojourn in the United States did much to promote Sino-American understanding, but her frankness had not always pleased the official cricles in Washington.[107]

Koo was then in the United States as China's chief delegate to the Dumbarton Oaks Conference. He was concerned over the worsening relationships between the two Allies. He exchanged views with H.H. K'ung, then Chiang's special envoy to the United States, Ambassador Wei Tao-ming, and many American leaders, including Congressman Walter Judd. On September 18, 1944, Koo sent a cable to Chiang, advising patience and tolerance in dealing with the United States, whose cooperation would be vitally important to China not only at the time of war but also for postwar reconstruction of the country.[108] The Chinese leadership fully appreciated the good intention of the United States, but the Stilwell incident eventually developed to such an extent that it became the most damaging factor in Sino-American relations.

Early in January 1942, Generalissimo Chiang accepted President Roosevelt's proposal to become the Supreme Commander of the China War Theater (including the area of Indochina and Thailand), with General Joseph W. Stilwell as Chiang's chief of staff. Instead of taking orders from Chiang, Stilwell had his own opinions on military operations, the distribution of lead-lease

---

[106] Further information on China's domestic situation at that time can be found in *Reminiscences of Wellington Koo,* Vol. V, p. 697.

[107] See *ibid.*, pp. 693-694.

[108] For details, see *ibid.*, pp. 688-694.

supplies, and the disposition of Chinese Communist forces. Due to policy differences and personality clashes, they could no longer work together. Finally, Chiang demanded Stilwell's recall, which was announced on October 25, 1944. President Roosevelt and General George C. Marshall tried very hard to keep Stilwell, whose final removal had adversely changed Washington's attitude toward China.

There have been divergent opinions on the Stilwell incident, and much has been written on the subject.[109] General Albert C. Wedemeyer, who succeeded Stilwell and won Chinese cooperation and friendship, attributed this unfortunate incident to the faults of Stilwell for "his gullibility concerning the Communists and his prejudicial view of Chiang Kai-shek and the Nationalist Government of China."[110]

China had long been resentful of British encroachments on her national sovereignty and territorial integrity since the middle of the nineteenth century. As allies, both governments had made attempts to improve their relations. As China's envoy to the Court of St. James for the second time in July 1941, Koo had left no stone unturned toward that end. The British goodwill mission arrived in Chungking on November 10, 1942, and had greatly helped the British public understand China. On December 3, 1943,

---

[109] Among these are Barbara Tuchman, *Stilwell and the American Experience in China, 1911-45* (New York: Macmillan, 1971); Chin-tung Liang, *General Stilwell in China, 1924-1944: The Full Story* (New York: St. John's University Press, 1972). See also *Reminiscences of Wellington Koo,* Vol. V, pp. 694-696.

[110] Albert C. Wedemeyer, *Wedemeyer Reports* (New York: Holt, 1958), p. 197.

the Chinese goodwill mission reached England for the promotion of mutual understanding. Soon afterward, Prime Minister Churchill dispatched Lt. General Carton de Wiart to Chungking as his special military representative to maintain close contacts with the Chinese government.[111]

There were, however, several major issues confronting the two countries. The most important one was strategic differences with respect to the execution of the war. Prime Minister Churchill was insistent on a policy of Europe-first on the ground that only when the victory over Germany was achieved, could the war in the Pacific be effectively pursued. In his view, to divide the attention and resources on two fronts at the same time would be disastrous. On the other hand, Generalissimo Chiang deemed that the war against Japan should be equally emphasized by the Allies. The final decision was made in Washington in favor of Europe-first strategy, with due assistance to China to continue her resistance against Japan.[112]

The problem of India's independence and the return of Hongkong to China generated much frictions between the two countries. Generalissimo Chiang regarded the Indian independence movement with favor. The Labor Party in England intended to give India dominion status, if not independence, right away. This view was not shared by the Conservative government, which was resentful of Chiang's visits with Mahatma Gandhi and Jawaharlal Nehru in February 1942. Churchill did not want to be the prime minister who would liquidate the British Empire. In his

---

[111] See *Reminiscences of Wellington Koo,* Vol. V, pp. 130, 197-239; *China Handbook,* 1937-1945, pp. 160-161.

[112] See *Reminiscences of Wellington Koo,* Vol. V, pp. 50-51.

conversation with Ambassador Koo, he mentioned that the Indian problem would be taken up when the victory was in sight.[113] The Hongkong issue was brought up soon after Koo's arrival in London. The general sentiment in Great Britain was that this Crown colony should be returned to China after the war. Upon Koo's recommendation, the Chinese government decided to postpone the discussion of the subject. In April 1945, when General Patrick J. Hurley was sent by President Roosevelt to talk with Prime Minister Churchill on the retrocession of Hongkong to China, the latter replied that the colony would be yielded "over my dead body."[114] On the other hand, China has always considered Hongkong as her *terra irrendenta* ever since it was ceded to England by the Treaty of Nanking of August 29, 1842, as a consequence of the Opium War.

Other disagreements included the diversion of labor and material to the construction of the Ledo Road (also known as the Stilwell Road) from Assam in India across upper Burma to China.[115] China was suspicious of British designs in Tibet. Unexpectedly, the British war loan to China had become a subject of frustrated negotiations. Following the lead of the United States, Foreign Secretary Anthony Eden telephoned Ambassador Koo on February 2, 1942, that the British government decided to grant a loan of fifty million pounds and also to allocate supplies of

---

[113] See *ibid.*, pp. 36-49. Nehru made a trip to Chungking in 1943 and another one in the early part of 1945. He was quite critical of Chiang's rule in China.

[114] *Ibid.*, p. 794. See also pp. 27-33, 1126, 1130.

[115] See *ibid.*, pp. 23-26.

munitions and military equipment on a lend-lease basis. Actually, the British treasury had no money to offer, and the factories could not be expected to manufacture much war equipment for other allies. In spite of prolonged discussions, China was able to get only a small portion of the loan.[116] Thus the Chinese government was much disappointed with this transaction.

In the British official circles, there were many friendly to China. Sir Stafford Cripps was one. Lady Cripps was most enthusiastic in her efforts to help China. At the same time, Chungking extended a warm welcome to Admiral Lord Louis Mountbatten, Supreme Commander of the Southeast Asia Command, when he went to confer with Generalissimo Chiang in March 1945. Madame Chiang was cordially invited by the King to visit England, but regrettably her health did not permit her to take the trip. Probably Sino-British relations might have been further improved if Madame Chiang had found it possible to meet Prime Minister Churchill to exchange views as earnestly hoped by President Roosevelt early in May 1943, when both of them were in the United States.[117] It had been Koo's conviction that China should maintain close cooperation with Great Britain and America (ABC alliance) during the period of war and in time of peace.

Mention should also be made of China's wartime relations with France, one of the major powers. No important issue existed between the two countries, except the leased territory of

---

[116]For details, see *ibid.*, pp. 13, 22, 114, 194-196, 301-302, 353-356, 550-551, 576, 608.

[117]See *ibid.*, pp. 247-249, 330, 337-339, 348-349, 406-410, 416-419, 422, 433, 437-438, 443-444, 454, 467-468, 471-493, 496, 740, 1120.

Kuangchouwan and transit facilities through Indochina as stated before. When Paris fell to Germany in June 1940, Koo was still Ambassador to France and went to Vichy prior to his transfer to London. The British government soon pledged its support of General de Gaulle and severed relations with the Vichy Government under Marshall Pétain. China extended recognition to the French Committee of National Liberation on August 28, 1943, and to the Provisional Government of France on October 23 of the following year. Diplomatic envoys were exchanged in due course, followed by cultural cooperation.

The Chinese section of the Yunnan-Indochina Railway was taken over by China on August 1, 1943, in accordance with the Sino-French Convention of April 9, 1898.[118] The rendition of the leased territory of Kuangchouwan took place on August 18, 1945.[119] As to the future of Indochina, President Roosevelt once sought Koo's view during their conversation in May 1944.[120] China had no territorial ambition in Indochina, but was deeply concerned with its future status because of its contiguity to her southwestern provinces and a large number of Chinese residents.

Owing to China's friendship with the United States and the close ties of Anglo-American relations, the Soviet Union had

---

[118] For its text, see MacMurray, *Treaties*, Vol. I, pp. 123-125, 128-130.

[119] See *China Handbook*, 1937-1945, pp. 174-176.

[120] See *Reminiscences of Wellington Koo*, Vol. V, pp. 449-452, 1195. President Roosevelt said to Koo that Indochina should not be returned to France, but should be administered by China and the United States, and possibly a third country, pending complete independence at a fixed date. See *ibid.*, p. 450.

always been concerned with political and economic domination in China by Western Democracies. To strengthen the Soviet position in China, Stalin had increased pressures in Sinkiang, set up a Communist regime in Outer Mongolia, and incorporated Tannu Tuva into Soviet territory. Chungking failed to win Moscow's friendship by offering proposals for trade and economic cooperation in January 1945. When H.H. K'ung and Koo were in New York in September 1944, they discussed at length how to improve Sino-Soviet relations and had their views made known to Generalissimo Chiang. President Roosevelt told K'ung that it was important for China to keep on good terms with the Soviet Union.[121] While seriously working toward that goal, China had never expected that President Roosevelt and Prime Minister Churchill would conclude an agreement with Marshal Stalin at the Yalta Conference (February 4-11, 1945), sacrificing China's sovereign rights and territorial integrity without her prior knowledge and consent.

Anxious to get Soviet participation in the war against Japan in order to save American lives,[122] President Roosevelt was willing to pay the price of Port Arthur and Dairen in Manchuria even before the Yalta Conference. As early as October 1944, Koo found out the American intention in Washington from Admiral William D. Leahy, Roosevelt's Chief of Staff, who was, however, well

---

[121] See *ibid.*, pp. 313-316, 678-681, 691-692.

[122] At that time, the United States government had already received reliable information of the imminent collapse of Japan through its intelligence reports of the three forces. See Herbert Feis, *The China Tangle: The American Effort in China from Pearl Harbor to the Marshall Mission* (Princeton: Princeton University Press, 1953), p. 236.

disposed to Koo's alternative proposal of giving some seaport on the coast of northeastern corner of Korea for Soviet use as the price of her independence from Japan. This conversation was reported to Generalissimo Chiang by Koo, but the Chinese government did not follow it up.[123] Then, on March 18, 1945, Chiang showed Koo in Chungking a cable from Wei Tao-ming, Chinese Ambassador to the United States, reporting his interview with President Roosevelt about the Yalta Agreement. Wei stated that Stalin indicated informally three conditions for Soviet entrance into the war against Japan: separation of Outer Mongolia from China, joint administration of the Chinese railways in Manchuria, and the special status of Port Arthur. Although Wei's report was rather vague, Koo advised Chiang that he should point out to Roosevelt the adverse consequences to the United States and China as well as all of East Asia if Stalin's terms were satisfied.[124]

It was only on June 15, 1945 that Presidnet Truman authorized Ambassador Patrick J. Hurley to inform Generalissimo Chiang of the exact terms of the Yalta Agreement,[125] which were more extensive than China had known before. In addition to Port Arthur, Moscow wanted another commercial port, Dairen, for its

---

[123] See *Reminiscences of Wellington Koo*, Vol. V, p. 1279.

[124] See *ibid.*, pp. 759-761.

[125] For its text, see Chen, *Treaties*, pp. 194-195. T. V. Soong, then Chinese Foreign Minister visited President Truman in May 1945, but the latter did not disclose the substance of the Yalta Agreement. See *Reminiscences of Wellington Koo*, Vol. V, p. 1079. For an analysis of the Yalta Agreement and its impact on China, see Tang Tsou, *America's Failure in China, 1944-50* (Chicago: University of Chicago Press, 1963), pp. 237-270.

use.[126] Historically, these two ports were leased to Russia by China in 1898 for twenty-five years, but were later transferred to Japan by Russia as one of the peace terms to terminate the Russo-Japanese War in 1905. This transaction, performed without the consent of the original lessor, had violated the 1898 Sino-Russian Convention.[127] The railways in Manchuria under the control of Japan or the puppet state Manchukuo should rightfully have been restored to China after the war.[128] As to Outer Mongolia, it was recognized as an integral part of China in Article V of the Sino-Soviet Agreement of May 31, 1924, which was concluded by Koo, then China's Foreign Minister, and Leo M. Karakhan, Soviet special envoy to Peking.[129]

---

[126]The problem of the seaports was discussed between President Truman and Marshal Stalin at Potsdam on July 17, 1945. See James F. Byrnes, *Speaking Frankly* (New York: Harper & Bros., 1947), p. 205.

[127]For the text of the Convention of March 27, 1898, see Chinese Customs, *Treaties,* Vol. I, pp. 219-226; MacMurray, *Treaties,* Vol. I, pp. 119-122.

[128]Among the terms of the Yalta Agreement was the establishment of a joint Soviet-Chinese company to operate the Chinese Eastern Railway and the Southern Manchurian Railway. The latter was constructed and operated by Japan; the former, originally under the joint ownership of China and Russia, but was arbitarily sold by Moscow to Manchukuo over Chinese protests. For details of the railway concessions in China, see William L. Tung, *China and the Foreign Powers*, pp. 116-123, 133-137.

[129]For an analysis of the Agreement, see *ibid.*, pp. 221-224, 240-241. The text of the Agreement can be found in League of Nations, *Treaty Series,* No. 955 (1925), Vol. 37, p. 176; Carnegie, *Treaties,* pp. 133-140. For the negotiations, see *Reminiscences of Wellington Koo,* Vol. III, pp. 453-483.

The three leaders at Yalta realized that the Chinese concessions "will require the concurrence of Generalissimo Chiang Kai-shek," but they agreed that "these claims of the Soviet Union shall be unquestionably fulfilled after Japan had been defeated." It was later confirmed that Foreign Secretary Eden was against this Agreement, but Prime Minister Churchill deemed that it was primarily an American affair.[130] According to the Agreement, the President of the United States had to "take measures in order to obtain this concurrence on advice from Marshal Stalin."[131] Under the circumstances, China was compelled to negotiate with the Soviet Union. T. V. Soong, President of the Executive *Yuan* (Prime Minister), led a delegation to discuss how to implement the Yalta terms with Stalin.[132] On August 14, 1945, the Sino-Soviet Treaty was signed between Wang Shih-chieh and Vyacheslav Molotov, Chinese and Soviet Foreign Ministers respectively.[133]

---

[130] See *ibid.*, Vol. V, p. 1191.

[131] Quotes from the Yalta Agreement. See Chen, *Treaties*, p. 195. For further information and comments, see Winston S. Churchill, *Triumph and Tragedy* (Boston: Houghton Mifflin, 1953), p. 390; John Leighton Stuart, *Fifty Years in China* (New York: Random House, 1954), pp. 177, 179, 180, 272, 313.

[132] For details of the negotiations, see *Reminiscences of Wellington Koo,* Vol. V, pp. 1104-1113. Further information can be found in Chin-tung Liang's paper "The Sino-Soviet Treaty of Friendship and Alliance of 1945: The Inside Story," delivered at the Conference on Wartime China, 1937-1945, held at Urbana, Illinois, on April 30 — May 2, 1976, under the joint sponsorship of the University of Illinois and St. John's University, New York.

[133] For the text of the Treaty and related documents, see Chinese

Prior to Soong's visit to Moscow, Koo advised him to exercise great caution in dealing with Soviet demands. In Koo's view, China should delay the negotiation with Moscow but hasten to solve the Nationalist-Communist disputes with a view to achieving domestic stability in opposition to external pressure.[134] The commitments made by President Roosevelt and Prime Minister Churchill at Yalta at the expense of China were much more unjust than the transfer of Shantung rights from Germany to Japan at the Paris Peace Conference. It was not until the Washington Conference (1921-1922) that the Shantung problem was settled at China's satisfaction. Nobody knows more than Koo how difficult it was to recover lost rights, because he himself was the spokesman for China's cause at both Paris and Washington.[135]

The eventual conclusion of the Sino-Soviet Treaty of 1945 might be motivated by a hope launched by the Chinese government to limit exactly how far Moscow could go and also by a vague promise on the part of the Soviet Union to support the National Government and to refrain from interfering in China's

---

Republic, *Treaties,* pp. 505-523; Chen, *Treaties,* pp. 218-234. For further comments on the implementation of the Yalta Agreement, see Tang Tsou, *op. cit.,* pp. 270-287.

[134] See *Reminiscences of Wellington Koo,* Vol. V, p. 1080.

[135] See *Reminiscences of Wellington Koo,* Vol. II, pp. 175, 197-208, 271-249, 265-295. For a summary of China's diplomatic efforts for the return of the Shantung rights, see William L. Tung, *China and the Foreign Powers,* pp. 160-163, 190-192. Dr. Koo's diplomatic encounters with President Wilson, Prime Minister Lloyd George, and Premier Georges Clemenceau were well described by Wunsz King in a booklet, entitled *Woodrow Wilson, Wellington Koo and the China Question at the Paris Peace Conference* (Leyden: A.W. Sythoff, 1959).

internal affairs.[136] But later events revealed that Stalin had not even observed this commitment. On February 25, 1953, long after the Communist victory on the mainland, the National Government in Taiwan declared the Treaty null and void because of Soviet failure to fulfill its obligations.[137]

---

[136] See Art. 5 of the Treaty and Arts. 2-3 of the Exchange of Notes.

[137] For the statement by the Foreign Minister of the Republic of China in Taiwan, see Chinese Republic, *Treaties,* pp. 523-524; Chen, *Treaties* pp. 233-234. The railway rights and the seaports were restored to China as a result of Peking's painful negotiations with Moscow. See William L. Tung, *China and the Foreign Powers,* pp.320-321.

CHAPTER SEVEN

Participation in the Establishment of International Organizations

The importance of international organizations to world peace and order has long been recognized by philosophers, publicists, and political writers. Many plans were formulated for the institution of representative bodies in the name of assembly or council composed of participating states.[138] The failure of the League of Nations was not due to its own faults but because of lack of resolute support from its constituent members. Before the end of World War II, the United States took the lead to establish several specilized agencies, all international in nature. These included the Food and Agriculture Organization in 1943, as well as the International Bank for Reconstruction and Development

---

[138]In the West, Dante Alighieri, Pierre Dubois, William Penn, and Jeremy Bentham were among the advocates. For details, see L.L. Leonard, *International Organization* (New York: McGraw-Hill, 1951), pp. 23-28.

and the International Monetary Fund in 1944. As a nation believing in international cooperation, China joined these organizations from the very beginning.

The Moscow Declaration of October 30, 1943 expressly recognized the urgent necessity of creating a new international organization of general nature.[139] In the fall of 1944, the United States government invited Great Britain, China, and the Soviet Union to send delegates to Dumbarton Oaks in Washington, D.C. for preliminary discussions of the subject. As signatories of the Moscow Declaration, the four powers had already prepared proposals for drafting a constitution of the future international organization. The Chinese government paid considerable attention to the American invitation and appointed its senior diplomat, Wellington Koo, Ambassador to Great Britain, to head the Chinese delegation to Dumbarton Oaks. As stated before, Koo was a member of the Drafting Committee of the Covenant of the League of Nations in 1919. The other Chinese delegates were Wei Tao-ming (Ambassador to the United States) and Victor Hoo (Vice Minister of Foreign Affairs).

At that time, Sino-Soviet relations were rapidly deteriorating. The Soviet Union insisted on holding two series of conferences on the ground that, unlike China, she was not at war with Japan: United States and Great Britain with the Soviet Union from August 21 to September 28, and with China from September 29 to October 7, 1944. The American government was then most conciliatory to Soviet demands. Facing a virtual *fait accompli,* Chinese participation became merely a gesture, even though some

---

[139] Art. 4 of the Moscow Declaration. See *Yearbook of the United Nations,* 1946-47, p. 3.

minor points were eventually incorporated into the draft agreed upon at the first phase of the conference. In fact, the final form of the Dumbarton Oaks proposals was not essentially different from China's original hopes.[140] Suprisingly, however, the Soviet draft of the communique announcing the result of the conference mentioned the agreement of three governments only, China not being considered as a great power equal to the other three. The British delegation was inclined to agree with the Soviet view. Of course, this differentiation was unacceptable to China. The issue was referred to Moscow, London, and Chungking. Finally, upon Koo's suggestion, any reference to three or four governments was eliminated from the communique.[141]

At the Moscow Conference, China was recognized as one of the four major powers. But, to Koo's great disappointment, "Dumbarton Oaks was a step backward in this respect."[142] China's international position had indeed been weakened by domestic disunity and military impotence in resisting Japan's advances. Under the circumstances prevailing at the time, a diplomat even with Koo's experience could not be expected to achieve a miracle. However, what Koo and the Chinese delegation had done in presenting China's case and contributing to the success of the conference had won the great admiration of the American delegation.[143]

---

[140] See *Reminiscences of Wellington Koo,* Vol. V, pp. 662-665.

[141] See *ibid.,* p. 661.

[142] *Ibid.,* p. 639.

[143] Dr. Stanley K. Hornbeck of the American delegation made such a

The Dumbarton Oaks Proposals as finally agreed upon by the four powers consisted of twelve chapters,[144] the essentials of which were later adopted by the Charter of the United Nations. However, several important questions remained to be settled, including the unanimity rule of the permanent members of the Security Council in reaching decisions on non-procedural matters, trusteeship of the League mandates and the colonies of enemy states, the issue of establishing a new international court or continuing the old one, and the problem of individual Soviet republics as initial members of the Organization.[145] These questions were later discussed and mainly resolved at the Yalta Conference on February 4–11, 1945.[146] As a concession to Stalin, Roosevelt and Churchill accepted Ukraine and Byelorussia as initial members. They agreed on the establishment of a trusteeship system and the exclusion of voting at the Security Council by a permanent member involved in a controversy in the nature of pacific settlement of disputes. An International Court of Justice was to be established as one of the six main organs of the United Nations. In this respect, the new court is different from its

---

complimentary remark to Dr. Hu Shih, former Chinese Ambassador to the United States. See *ibid.*, p. 665.

[144] The text of the Proposals can be found in *Yearbook of the United Nations,* 1946-47, pp. 4-9; *Dumbarton Oaks Documents on International Organization,* Department of State Conference Series 56, publication 2192.

[145] For details, see William L. Tung, *International Organization under the United Nations System.* pp. 29-30.

[146] For the text of the Yalta Agreement on matters relating to the United Nations, see *Yearbook of the United Nations,* 1946-47, pp. 9-10.

predecessor, the Permanent Court of International Justice, which was an autonomous body, not a principal organ of the League of Nations.

China's status as a major power, while unsuccessfully challenged by the Soviet Union at Dumbarton Oaks, was reaffirmed at San Francisco. Great Britain, the United States, the Soviet Union, and China became four Sponsoring Powers of the United Nations Conference on International Organization, held at San Francisco, from April 25 to June 26, 1945. For the preparation of the conference and consultations with the Chinese government on other matters, Koo arrived in Chungking on March 1. Because of the domestic situation in China, Koo persistently recommended that a Communist member be included in the Chinese delegation. The Nationalist leadership, while initially unfavorable to the appointment of non-diplomats to participate in international conferences, finally decided to have several members of other political parties and a few independents as Chinese delegates to the San Francisco Conference as a demonstration of national unity.[147]

The Chinese delegation was composed of ten members; only four of them were closely affiliated with the government, namely, T.V. Soong (Foreign Minister), Wellington Koo (Ambassador to Great Britain), C.H. Wang (Secretary-General of the Supreme National Defense Council,) and Wei Tao-ming (Ambassador to the United States). As representatives of the three minor parties were

---

[147]In his cable to Generalissimo Chiang Kai-shek dated March 15, 1945, President Roosevelt expressed the desirability to include members of the Communist Party or other political parties as Chinese delegates to the San Francisco Conference. See *Reminiscences of Wellington Koo*, Vol. V, pp. 773-774.

Tung Pi-wu (a senior leader of the Chinese Communist Party),[148] Carsun Chang (founder of the China Democratic Socialist Party), and Li Huang (a senior leader of the China Youth Party). The other three were generally known as independents: Hu Shih (an eminent scholar and former Ambassador to the United States), Wu Yi-fang (President of Ginling Women's College in Nanking), and Wang Yun-wu (President of the Commercial Press). Wu was the only woman member. Wang was also a member of the Presidium of the People's Political Council.[149] Soong as Foreign Minister was titular head of the delegation. He took the conference rather lightly, leaving it entirely to Koo with himself negotiating financial and other matters with the American government.[150] In view of the divergent backgrounds of the Chinese delegates, Koo exerted maximum efforts to coordinate their working relationships. With a single exception, they all spoke in one voice at the conference.[151]

---

[148]Koo had a favorable impression of Tung Pi-wu, and considered him qualified to be a delegate in his reply to an inquiry by government authorities. Recalling Tung's visit with him at the Chinese Embassy in Paris, Koo frankly stated: "I had no enmity toward any group, as I believed that there was no one line of political thought which could be absolutely right to the exclusion of others." *Ibid.*, p. 808.

[149]The People's Political Council was more or less a representative body in wartime China. For its origin, membership, organization, and functions, see Ch'ien Tuan-sheng, *The Government and Politics of China* (Cambridge: Harvard University Press, 1950), pp. 280-295; William L. Tung, *The Political Institutions of Modern China*, pp. 188-192.

[150]See *Reminiscences of Wellington Koo*, Vol. V, p. 804.

[151]Koo felt that the working relationships among the Chinese delegates at San Francisco were even better than those at Paris and

Despite preliminary discussions at Dumbarton Oaks and Yalta, the United States and the Soviet Union frequently disagreed on various subjects at the conference, such as the establishment of a strategic area under the trusteeship system, recognition of regional arrangements, and provision of enforcement measures. Throughout the meetings, Koo tried to promote conciliation and compromise.[152] He was generally sympathetic with many reasonable expectations of small states. This had been his consistent attitude from the time when he was a member of the Covenant Drafting Committee at the Paris Peace Conference in 1919.[153] As the proceedings and resolutions of the conference are of public record, it is unnecessary to give the details here.[154] The Charter of the United Nations was adopted on June 26, 1945, when the five permanent members of the Security Council and a majority of other member states completed the procedure of

---

Washington conferences. According to Koo's recollection, Li Huang once failed to comply with the delegation rule by criticizing the Nationalist Party in an interview with a foreign correspondent. Actually, however, Li intended only to explain the history and policy of the China Youth Party. See *ibid.*, pp. 797-798, 815-816.

[152] For details, see *ibid.*, pp. 832-840.

[153] Colonel Edward M. House once said that Koo's appeal on behalf of the small powers was the best he had ever heard at the Committee. See *ibid.*, p. 663.

[154] Reference may be made to *Documents of the United Nations Conference on International Organization, San Francisco, 1945* (New York: United Nations Information Service, 1945-1946), 22 vols.

ratification.[155] In evaluating Koo's work at the conference, it is better to quote what Secretary of State Stettinius said about the former's "many contributions on many committees whose delicate situations called for tactful handling."[156] When President Truman saw Koo at the end of the conference, he sincerely reiterated the complimentary remarks made by his Secretary of State.[157]

In accordance with the Interim Arrangements signed by the delegates at the San Francisco Conference on June 26, 1945, a Preparatory Commission was established to work out necessary procedures for the first session of the General Assembly of the United Nations. The actual responsibility fell on its Executive Committee of fourteen.[158] Koo represented China on the Committee.[159] When the first session of the General Assembly was convened in London on Janurry 10, 1946, Koo once more led the Chinese delegation and contributed his experience and skill to this

---

[155] For the text of the United Nations Charter, of which the Statute of the International Court of Justice is an integral part, see *Yearbook of the United Nations,* 1946-47, pp. 831-850. An analysis of the theory and practice of the Charter can be found in Leland M. Goodrich and Edvard Hambro, *Charter of the United Nations: Commentary and Documents.* Boston: World Peace Foundation, rev. ed., 1949).

[156] *Reminiscences of Wellington Koo,* Vol. V, p. 1086.

[157] *Loc. cit.*

[158] The Executive Committee was set up by the first session of the Preparatory Commission, held at San Francisco, on June 27, 1945. See *Yearbook of the United Nations,* 1946-47, pp. 35-36.

[159] See *Reminiscences of Wellington Koo,* Vol. V, p. 1197.

newly-born semi-legislative body of the world.[160] Thus, in his lifetime, Koo witnessed and actively participated in the founding of the two international organizations.

---

[160]The second part of the first session of the General Assembly was held in New York, from October to December 1946. Koo had been transferred from London to Washington as Chinese Ambassador to the United States in July 1946, and continued to lead the Chinese delegation to participate in the deliberations of the first session of the General Assembly. See *ibid.*, Vol. VI, pp. Al, A40-A46. As the scope of this paper is limited to China's wartime diplomacy, Koo's postwar activities in Washington and New York are not discussed here.

CHAPTER EIGHT

China's Diplomacy and Diplomats

Diplomacy is the conduct of foreign affairs through peaceful means by a state for the execution of its foreign policies.[161] Government officials in charge of diplomacy serving either at home or abroad are generally called diplomats. The most important functions of an envoy are representation, protection, negotiation, and observation. As a representative of a sending state, he should endeavor to promote friendly relations with the receiving state, to protect the rights and interests of his own country and its nationals, to observe conditions and developments from his post, and, above all, to conduct negotiations for the furtherance of its national goals.[162] In the foreign office, the

---

[161]There are as many definitions of "diplomacy" as text writers. See Ernest Satow, *A Guide to Diplomatic Practice* (London: Longmans, Green & Co., 4th ed., 1957, edited by Sir Nevile Bland), pp. 1-2.

[162]For details, see William L. Tung, *International Law in an*

minister and his top aides have the responsibility of deciding policies and directing the missions abroad for their implementation. Thus the qualifications required of a diplomat are quite high, and his success depends much on his training, experience, and devotion.

In external relations, a state, strong or weak, relies heavily on skillful diplomacy, because war is only the last resort to settle international disputes and any compulsory means even short of war frequently results in adverse consequences. Since the emergence of the state system, Europe has produced many celebrated diplomats to meet the complicated situation in a comparatively small area crowded with large and small nations. Machiavelli, Metternich, and Talleyrand were only a few of these renowned figures before the turn of the century.

During the Chou dynasty (c.11th century-221 B.C.), particularly the periods of the so-called Spring and Autumn (770-475 B.C.) and Warring States (475-221 B.C.), interstate relationships in China had necessitated delicate negotiations undertaken by tactful diplomats. History has also recorded quite a number of talented politicians and military strategists entrusted by the emperors with diplomatic missions to China's neighbors. Nevertheless, due to her predominance in Asia and long isolation from the rest of the world, diplomacy in the modern sense had not caught the attention of the Chinese rulers until the conclusion of the Treaty of Nerchinsk with Russia on August 27, 1689, for the demarcation of boundaries, extradition of fugitives, and regulation

---

Organizing World, pp. 251-254. Further information on the subject of diplomatic relations can be found in *ibid.*, Ch. 9.

of trade on a reciprocal basis.[163]

The nineteenth century was characterized by Western imperialism and colonialism. Taking advantage of China's internal weakness and military unpreparedness in the 1840's, Great Britain, followed by other powers, used force and other means to obtain territorial, political, economic, and administrative concessions, as well as extraterritorial jurisdiction from China.[164] The Sino-British Treaty of August 29, 1842,[165] for the termination of the Opium War, set a precedent of unequal treaties imposed on China. Following the footsteps of Western powers, Japan had continuously carried out aggressions in China; unlike the former, however, the latter never learned when and where to stop. Thus the major task of Chinese diplomats had been the resistance to

---

[163] For its text, see *Treaties and Conventions between China and Foreign States* (Shanghai: Statistical Department of the Inspector General of the Chinese Maritime Customs, 2d ed., 1917, 2 vols., covering the period 1689-1915, with texts in Chinese and other languages; hereafter cited as Chinese Customs, *Treaties*), Vol. I, pp. 3-13; *Treaties, etc., between Great Britain and China; between China and Foreign Powers; and Orders in Council, Rules, Regulations, Acts of Parliament, Decrees, etc., Affecting British Interests in China* (edited by Edward Hertslet, 3rd ed. by Godfrey E. P. Hertslet, covering the period 1689-1907, 2 vols., London: Harison & Sons, 1908; hereafter cited as Hertslet, *Treaties*), Vol. I, pp. 437-439.

[164] For details, see William L. Tung, *China and the Foreign Powers*, Chs. 2-5; W. W. Willoughby, *Foreign Rights and Interests in China* (Baltimore: Johns Hopkins Press, 1972, 2 vols.), Vol. I, pp. 1-8. It should be noted that the early traders from the West failed to give China a good impression. See V. K. Wellington Koo, *The Status of Aliens in China* (New York: Columbia University Press, 1912), p. 64.

[165] For the text of the Treaty, see Chinese Customs, *Treaties*, Vol. I, pp. 351-356; Hertslet, *Treaties*, Vol. I, pp. 7-12.

Japan's encroachment and invasion, as well as the abrogation of unequal treaties.

Because of great reluctance of the Imperial Court of the Ch'ing dynasty, a central office to conduct foreign relations was not set up until 1861. First known as Tsungli Yamen (Tsung-li Ko-kuo Shih-wu Yamen), it was reorganized in 1901 into Wai-wu Pu, which was renamed Wai-chia Pu (Ministry of Foreign Affairs) after the inauguration of the Republic in 1912. Although special missions had been sent abroad since 1866, it had to wait eleven years more to establish the first permanent legation in London and then other legations in Tokyo and Berlin.[166]

Despite her late start, China had nevertheless produced many first-rate diplomats in the twentieth century. Three of them were even senior to Wellington Koo: W.W. (Wei-ching) Yen (Prime Minister; Foreign Minister; Minister to the United States, Germnay, Sweden, and Denmark; Ambassador to the Soviet Union), Alfred (Sao-ke) Sze (Minister to Great Britain; Minister and later Ambassador to the United States; Foreign Minister, appointed but having not taken up the office), and C.H. (Chung-hui) Wang (Prime Minister; Foreign Minister; and Judge of the Permanent Court of International Justice). They also represented China at international conferences and organizations. Among Koo's other contemporaries were F.T. (Tien-hsi) Cheng (Ambassador to Great Britain; Judge of the Permanent Court of International Justice), Tai-chi Quo (Ambassador to Great Britain;

---

[166] For details, see William L. Tung, *China and Some Phases of International Law*, Chs. V—VI; Knight Biggerstaff, "The Establishment of Permanent Chinese Diplomatic Missons Abroad," *Chinese Social and Political Science Review*, Vol. 20 (April 1936), pp. 1-41.

Foreign Minister; Permenent Representative to the United Nations), Hsu Mo (Vice Minister of Foreign Affairs; Minister to Australia; Ambassador to Turkey; Judge of the International Court of Justice), and T.F. (Ting-fu) Tsiang (Ambassador to the Soviet Union and the United States; Permanent Representative to the United Nations).[167] Non-career diplomats, such as Hu Shih (Ambassador to the United States), also helped the government perform valuable functions at the time of national emergency. But none of them had served the country so long in so many important capacities as Wellington Koo, who, as a matter of fact, has outlived all of them.

Koo's unique achievements are attributed to his early language training, comprehensive knowledge of international affairs,[168] vast experience in diplomatic negotiations, and absolute devotion to his duties. He was determined to do his best in winning international support against Japan's intrusions and recovering China's sovereign rights by the termination of unequal treaties. Having no political ambition, he was ever willing to work for the legal government representing China. Ever since Japan forced President Yuan Shih-k'ai to accept the notorious Twenty-One Demands, Koo had engaged in many diplomatic battles against the aggressor at conference tables in Paris, Washington, and Geneva. The day after Japan's surrender to the Allied powers, Koo noted

---

[167]The list is, of course, by no means complete, because many other diplomats not mentioned here have also made due contributions.

[168]Reflecting on his studies at Columbia University in 1910's, Koo stated: "I had always been interested in diplomatic relations and had wanted to improve the conduct of China's foreign affairs, but I wasn't very keen on entering official life." *Reminiscences of Wellington Koo,* Vol. I, p. 130.

in his diary on August 15, 1945: "At last the moment to which I had been looking forward and about which I had dreamed and worked has arrived. Ever since I was seven years old when I heard with the depressed heart the news of China's defeat by Japan, I had desired to work for China's recovery and the removal of the Japanese menace."[169]

With respect to the termination of unequal treaties, Koo had repeatedly presented China's case at the Paris Peace Conference in 1919 and the Washington Conference in 1921-1922. As a consequence of World War I, Germany and Austria lost their special rights in China. The first act of terminating unequal treaties through diplomatic channel was performed by Koo, who as Foreign Minister concluded with Soviet special envoy Leo M. Karakhan the Agreement on General Principles for the Settlement of the Questions, with Six Declarations and Exchange of Notes, on May 31, 1924.[170] Among other things, this Agreement contained the following provisions: annulment of all conventions, treaties, agreements, protocols, contracts, etc. concluded between China

---

[169] *Ibid.*, Vol. V, pp. 1103-1104. In celebrating the V-J Day, Koo (Ambassador to Great Britain) and the presnet writer (Ambassador to the Netherlands government then in exile in London) held a joint reception in the Chinese Embassy in London, attended by over eight hundred dignitaries. They included Attlee, Molotov, Bidault, and many cabinet ministers of the British and Netherlands governments, as well as diplomatic envoys then residing in London. Foreign Minister Wang Shih-chieh, then attending the Foreign Ministers Conference, naturally participated in the reception, but surprisingly Prime Minister T. V. Soong stayed away even though he was at the Embassy. See *ibid.*, Vol. V, pp. 1138-1139; William L. Tung, *Revolutionary China: A Personal Account, 1926-1945*, pp. 279-280.

[170] For its text, see League of Nations, *Treaty Series,* No. 955 (1925), Vol. 37, p. 176; Carnegie, *Treaties*, pp. 133-140.

Dr. Koo as Judge of the International Court of Justice at The Hague, 1957-1967; Vice President, 1964-1967.

Dr. Koo and Mrs. Juliana Koo at Tappen Hill, New York, 1959.

Dr. Koo with other Judges of the International Court of Justice, at The Hague, 1957.

On the occasion of Dr. Koo's presentation of his memoirs to Columbia University, on May 28, 1976, with President William J. McGill and Professor C. Martin Wilbur on the left.

Dr. and Mrs. Koo with the author and Mrs. Tung, on the same occasion as above, May 28, 1976.

90

and the Czarist government; negotiation for new ones "on the basis of equality, reciprocity, and justice, as well as the spirit of the Declaration of the Soviet Government of the years 1919 and 1920",[171] Soviet promise to terminate all treaties, agreements, etc. concluded between the Czarist government and any third party or parties which affected the sovereign rights or interests of China, and mutual guarantee not to conclude any treaties or agreements prejudicial to the sovereign rights or interests of either of them.[172] In spite of the deteriorating relationships between the two countries in later years, the Koo-Karakhan Agreement was epoch-making.

Another courageous move made by Koo was the renunciation of the Sino-Belgian Treaty of November 2, 1865, [173] by which Belgium obtained some unilateral rights and privileges in China through the application of the most-favored-nation clause. Since the Treaty was to expire on November 2, 1926, the Chinese government notified the Belgian government of its intention to conclude a new one to replace the old. The Belgian government argued that, according to Article 46 of the Treaty, only Belgium had the right to ask for a revision. When Koo resumed the portfolio of foreign affairs in October 1926, he took charge of

---

[171] Art. III of the Agreement.

[172] Art. IV of the Agreement. For the text of the first Karakhan Declaration of 1919, see Jane Degras (ed.), *Soviet Documents on Foreign Policy* (London: Oxford University Press, 1951, 3 vols.), Vol. I, pp. 92-93. His second Declaration of 1920 can be found in *The China Yearbook*, 1924-1925, pp. 870-872.

[173] For the text of the Treaty, see Chinese Customs, *Treaties*, Vol. II, pp. 4-22; Hertslet, *Treaties*, Vol. I, pp. 223-234.

this matter personally. Because no agreement could be reached on Koo's proposal of signing a *modus vivendi* pending the negotiation for a new treaty, the Chinese government promulgated a mandate on November 6, 1926, terminating the Treaty of 1865.

Challenging the legal validity of the doctrine of *rebus sic stantibus* as advocated by China,[174] the Belgian government submitted the dispute to the Permanent Court of International Justice.[175] The case was later withdrawn after the conclusion of a new treaty based on the principle of equality and reciprocity on November 22, 1928[176] Koo recalled that his decision of 1926 "was a landmark in Chinese diplomatic history, because it was the first time that an unequal treaty was declared completely abrogated by China in the face of the open and official opposition of the other party in the treaty."[177] However, the new treaty concluded by Foreign Minister C.T. Wang of the National Government in 1928 was the result of a compromise between the two contending parties. The Belgian government recognized the Chinese right of tariff autonomy, but still maintained extraterritorial jurisdiction in China until the majority of states enjoying that right would agree to its relinquishment.

---

[174] For divergent views and practices of this doctrine relating to vital change of circumstances, see William L. Tung, *International Law in an Organizing World*, pp. 356-359.

[175] See *Publications of the Permanent Court of International Justice,* Series A., No. 8.

[176] For its text, see League of Nations, *Treaty Series,* Vol. 87 (1929), pp. 287-295; Chinese Republic, *Treaties,* pp. 1923.

[177] *Reminiscences of Wellington Koo,* Vol. III, p. 499.

Thus Koo's life-long hope of abrogating unequal treaties had not been wholly fulfilled until the United States and Great Britain led the other countries to give up their extraterritorial jurisdiction by the conclusion of new treaties with China on January 11, 1943. As stated before, Koo was then in Chungking and actively participated in the negotiation for the conclusion of the Sino-British treaty. After the signing ceremony, Foreign Minister T.V. Soong said to Koo that "the treaty was really an epoch-making event, the greatest treaty of which China had been a party in the century."[178]

Question has been often raised about the tactics countributing to Koo's success in negotiations. First of all, he studied the conditions of the contracting parties most carefully. Then, in order to reach an agreement, he believed in conciliation and compromise, with due regard to China's sovereign rights and the interests of the others. In his opinion, the Chinese saying that it would be better to have a broken jade rather than a whole tile is an invaluable precept for personal life but not always applicable to diplomacy. This is particularly true in the case of negotiating a multilateral treaty.[179] It does not mean to make so much concession as to be detrimental to the interests of hiw own country. When the situation demanded, Koo did not hesitate to take resolute action. Among such instances was China's refusal to sign the Treaty of Versailles of 1919, when the Paris Peace Conference arbitrarily decided to transfer the Shantung rights to Japan as previously described.

---

[178] *Ibid.*, Vol. V. p. 293.

[179] See *ibid.*, Vol. V, pp. 1132A-1134.

Perhaps mention should also be made of a well-known case of Koo's dismissal of Sir Francis Aglen, then Inspector General of the Chinese Customs. It was then a general practice of the investment circles in China to obtain the approval of the Inspector General on any loan issue secured on the customs revenue in one form or another. When the Peking government wanted to raise a loan on the Austrian Boxer indemnity in the fall of 1926, Sir Francis was on home leave in England. Instead of complying with the government order to return to Peking right away, he delayed his journey by travelling around in South and Central China. Upon his arrival in Peking in January 1927, he refused to give signature to the loan. At that time, Koo was Prime Minister and concurrently Foreign Minister. The matter was laid before the Cabinet, and it was unanimously decided to dismiss Sir Francis because of his insubordination, to the surprise of banking and diplomatic circles in China.

In those days, the Inspector General of Customs, presumably representing British interests, was virtually regarded as the super minister of finance in China. In spite of the protest by the British Minister Sir Miles Lampson, this incident passed without great difficulties, and further strengthened Koo's conviction that "if China stood on her legitimate rights, her action, no matter how striking or even shocking it might appear in the Far East or Asia in general, would be fully understood abroad."[180] W.W. Yen, one of China's foremost diplomats and a former prime minister and foreign minister, considered this episode "as of interest and importance in the history of China's studied efforts to safeguard

---

[180]*Ibid.*, Vol. III, p. 422. Sir Francis was later succeeded by his Chief Secretary Edwards.

her rights of sovereignty and self-respect."[181]

Doubt was sometimes expressed about the extent of Koo's actual role in the decision-making process of China's foreign policy. Generally speaking, diplomats under the Peking government had more to say concerning its formulation and execution. When the Nationalist Party came to power in 1928, many of its leaders had previously received modern education abroad and were naturally more inclined to make decisions by themselves. In other words, Chinese diplomats under the National Government have taken less initiatives and normally acted under instructions.[182] There are, of course, exceptions. Koo had constantly made recommendations to the government on various problems arising in different parts of the world.[183] Because of his high prestige, comprehensive experience, and unusual resourcefulness, Koo's counsel had often been sought by the government during the course of decision-making. It is needless to say that his proposals had carried much weight.

The evaluation of Koo's diplomatic contributions to China would not be complete without briefly mentioning some of his postwar activities which were actually interwoven with his wartime career. Owing to the increasing importance of Sino-American relations, Koo was transferred from Great Britain

---

[181] W.W. Yen, *East-West Kaleidoscope, 1877-1944* (New York: St. John's University Press, 1974), Preface by V.K. Wellington Koo, p. x.

[182] For Koo's analysis of the conduct of foreign affairs between the governments in Peking and Nanking, see *Reminiscences of Wellington Koo*, Vol. III, pp. 556-574.

[183] See *ibid.*, Vol. IV, Preliminary Draft, pp. 348, 445-447.

to the United States soon after World War II to conduct complicated negotiations for American aid.[184] During his decade in Washington, the National Government had to move from Nanking to Canton and finally to Taiwan as a result of military defeat by the Communists. For a time, the ambassador and his staff worked on a reduced budget and even delayed payment of their salaries and allowances due to the financial difficulties of the government.[185] Notwithstanding such hardships, Koo had successfully fulfilled his responsibilities under most trying circumstances and commanded tremendous respect from the host country. Secretary of State John Foster Dulles was so disappointed with Koo's final decision of retirement in March 1956 that he even intended to persuade the Chinese government not to accept his resignation for the simple reason that it would be extremely difficult to find a man as his replacement.[186]

---

[184]The present writer was Adviser to the Foreign Minister and concurrently Director of American Affairs during the period of 1947-1948. Negotiating with the American Embassy, in Nanking for American aid to China, he fully understood and appreciated the difficulty of Ambassador Koo's task in Washington. See William L. Tung, *Revolutionary China: A Personal Account, 1926-1945*, pp. 293-315.

[185]Ambassador Koo and the present writer seriously discussed the matter and made various attempts to relieve the situation in December 1949, when the latter, as Vice Minister of Foreign Affairs, took an inspection trip abroad and visited Washington, D.C. See *ibid.*, pp. 370-385; *Reminiscences of Wellington Koo*, Vol. VI, pp. J309-J310.

[186]Of course, Koo immediately dissuaded Dulles from doing so. Approaching seventy years of age, Koo decided to retire from the Washington post, which had been very taxing to his health. To express his deep appreciation to Koo's "notable contribution," Dulles wrote that "my regret to

Koo became so indispensable to the Chinese government that, upon his resignation from the Washington post, he was immediately asked to be Ambassador at Large to undertake such goodwill and special missions as his health would permit. The government hoped Koo would take a trip to England right away for the purpose of improving relationships between Taipei and London. Generalissimo Chiang Kai-shek thought that Koo would be the best man to perform the task, because he had known Prime Minister Anthony Eden and many British cabinet ministers for a number of years. It is true that, when Koo was twice Chinese envoy to the Court of St. James, he had made a good impression in the official circles and with the general public. Indeed, as a diplomat, Koo's expertise had been well recognized. For instance, on one formal occasion in 1943, Eden said: "How very fortunate," the British government was in having Koo as Ambassador, "in the best sense of the word."[187] Chiefly on the ground of health, however, Koo declined the offer of the Chinese government.[188]

If the Chinese government had to comply with Koo's wish to

---

your decision to retire from your country's diplomatic service is particularly keen because of our long record of personal association, going back 37 years to the Versailles Conference." In this respect, Dulles emphasized that "I treasure the memories of this association." *Ibid.*, Vol. VII, p. L142. For further information on Koo's resignation see *ibid.*, pp. L110-L147.

[187] The occasion was at an official dinner on July 28, 1943, presided over by Eden on behalf of the British government in honor of Foreign Minister T.V. Soong. It was attended by members of the British war cabinet and the services, the American Ambassador, and many other leading figures. See *ibid.*, Vol. V, p. 563.

[188] See *ibid.*, Vol. VII, pp. L112-L116.

retire from ambassadorship, the United Nations and particularly the International Court of Justice would be gratified at having a man of his stature for international service. When Koo had hardly settled down in New York, the Chinese government wanted to nominate him as judge of this highest court of the world to succeed Judge Hsu Mo, who died at The Hague. It was mid-summer of 1956.[189] Since the work of a judge would not be as demanding as that of an ambassador to the United States, Koo agreed to the proposal of his nomination. In January 1957, Koo was elected concurrently by the Security Council and General Assembly of the United Nations.[190] For one decade, Koo served with distinction as Judge (1957-1967) and later also Vice President (1964-1967) of the International Court of Justice.[191]

While it is hardly possible to evaluate V.K. Wellington Koo as a diplomat without occasionally dwelling upon his whole career,[192] space does not permit elaboration of his postwar

---

[189] See *ibid.*, Vol. VIII, pp. 5-13.

[190] Koo's term was to fill out the remainder of Judge Hsu Mo's, but he was reelected to serve another full term. See *ibid.*, pp. 13-19. For the procedures of the election, see Arts. 2-12 of the Statute of the International Court of Justice (*Yearbook of the United Nations*, 1946-47, pp. 843-850).

[191] For Koo's work at The Hague, see *Reminiscences of Wellington Koo,* Vol VIII, pp. 23-41.

[192] Mention should also be made of another of Koo's appointments. When he turned down the offer by the Chinese government to be ambassador at large, he was earnestly urged to accept an honorary office of Senior Adviser to President Chiang Kai-shek. While this office implied no particular work, Koo resigned from it after being elected Judge of the International Court of Justice, in accordance with Art. 16, Para. 1 of its Statute. See

achievements. What has been described above should be sufficient to show how valuable Dr. Koo's contributions have been to his own country and to the furtherance of world order throughout his lifetime. There is no doubt that history will record him as the most accomplished diplomat modern China has ever produced.

Reminiscences of Wellington Koo, Vol. VII, p. L116; Vol. VIII, pp. 32-33.

Appendices

APPENDIX I

Speech By His Excellency Dr. V. K. Wellington Koo
Before the XVIIIth Assembly of the
League of Nations,
September 15, 1937

In the general discussion of the Secretary-Generals's annual report in the past, it has been a custom for the delegates to refer to the important events of world interest or international concern taking place in the year under review. Following this custom I wish to invite your attention to a situation of the gravest kind which has recently arisen in the Far East. Indeed I feel it my duty to inform you of it because of its utmost gravity pregnant with dire consenquences to the peace of the world.

Since two months ago my country has been once more subjected to armed aggression from Japan. The Japanese Government has despatched to China more than 300,000 troops, scores of warships, and hundreds of military aeroplanes in pursuit of political domination and territorial conquest. The Japanese Army, equipped with the most deadly instruments of war, has attacked and occupied Tientsin, Peiping, Naukow and Kalgan in the North, and is continuing to penetrate further into the interior of the country. In the South it has

Japanese Army of Invasion in China — 300,000 men

been attempting, with the aid of Japan's mighty fleet, to seize Shanghai, the great metropolis of the Far East. The Japanese Navy has declared an illegal blockade of the entire coast of China and the Japanese warplanes have systematically been carrying out air raids on cities and towns in thirteen provinces, some of which lie hundreds of miles inland. China, notwithstanding all her handicaps, has found herself obliged to resist this renewed armed invasion. A bitter conflict between the ruthless invaders who seek to impose their will by force and the determined defenders who wish to save their country and protect their people is raging at this very moment. Peace has been and remains gravely disturbed.

The systematic destruction of life and property by the Japanese invaders has been appalling. I do not wish to weary you with details but let me emphasize the horrible character of the deliberate attacks by Japanese warplanes on unarmed civilians.

Japanese Air Force — Bombs Chinese civilians

In Tientsin the most crowded parts of the Chinese city were bombed by Japanese aeroplanes killing hundreds of people at a time for no reason other than to terrorize the civilians. The sight of the mangled bodies and the cries of the maimed and wounded were so sickening to the hearts of the foreign Red Cross doctors that they voiced their fervent wish that the Governments of the civilised Powers would make an effort to stop the carnage.

The bombing of the civilian population in the

South has been even more frequent and horrible than in North China. One Japanese air raid on a Chinese railway station south of the French Concession in Shanghai killed hundreds of Chinese refugees, mostly women and children, waiting for a train to take them to their homes in the interior of the country for safety. The place was not a military base, nor were there troops present.

Here is a brief description of a froeign witness, the correspondent of the *Daily Mail,* who cabled to his paper under date of September 9th, less than a week ago: "The shrieks and cries of Chinese mothers rent the air yesterday at Sungkiang, near Shanghai as, with tear-filled eyes and dazed mien, they stumbled among the charred wreckage of a bombed refugee train, hunting for the mangled corpses of their children. At least three hundred people were killed and 400 more wounded when Japanese warplanes swooped down and bombed the train wrecking five carriages."

The bombing of the unprotected city of Changshu, 80 miles from the coast, killed 2,000 civilians. Nanking, the capital, has been subjected to almost daily raids by the Japanese air force, levying a frightful toll of deaths among the civilian population.

The systematic burning and demolition of schools, colleges, hospitals, Red Cross units and other cultural and humanitarian centres is sheer vandalism. As an illustration, let me refer to the case of Nankai University, one of the largest and

Demolishes cultural and educational institutions

best known private endowed educational instutions in North China. Japanese artillery wantonly turned its fire on the buildings of the University and Japanese warplanes dropped incendiary bombs on them. When the Japanese military authorities saw that the concrete structures had not been entirely razed to the ground, they burned them with oil and blew them up with dynamite.

Japanese using International Settlement as base of operations — loss of foreign life and property

As a result of the Japanese making use of the International Settlement as the base of their military operations to attack the Chinese in Shanghai, foreign life and property have also suffered and are still suffering grievous losses. Scores of innocent foreigners have been killed or wounded. Foreign ships of commerce and war have been hit and damaged by bombs or shrapnels. Foreign plants, mills, warehouses and office buildings have been occupied by Japanese troops. Seventy thousand foreign residents have been obliged to evacuate the city. The illegal blockade of the Chinese coast proclaimed by the Japanese fleet has been interfering with foreign as well as Chinese ships entering Chinese ports for lawful trade. The menace of Japanses aggression to life and property has been so serious that even the Ambassador of a great and friendly Power travelling on business in a private automobile at a distance of 50 miles from Shanghai was bombed and machine-gunned by two Japanese warplanes.

In a word, the situation in the Far East today is one of the gravest character. Japan in the grip of a ruthless war party has openly resorted to force as an instrument of policy and let loose its gigantic and powerful war machine to seek domination and conquest of China on the Asiatic mainland.

It may be asked what were the circumstances which had led to the outbreak of the present hostilities between China and Japan. A full answer is given in two statements which the Chinese Government sent to the Secretary-General of the League of Nations on August 30th and September 12th, and which have been distributed to the Governments of the Member States of the League and to the Advisory Committee of the Assembly on the Far Eastern situation, including the United States. It is unnecessary for me to go into details here; let me merely point out the fact that the Lukouchiao incident, which the Japanese seized as a pretext for starting large scale military operations in North China, was not much different from many other incidents of Japanese provocation, including the one by which the Japanese claimed to justify their attack on Mukden in the night of September 18th, 1931, and their subsequent occupation of whole Manchuria.

Briefly, the facts are these. In the evening of July 7th Japanese troops held illegal maneuvers at Lukouchiao, a railway junction of strategic importance ten miles south of Peiping, where their presence could not be defended under any existing treaty or agreement. Alleging that one of their soldiers was missing, the Japanese troops demand-

Origin of conflict July 7th

ed after midnight to enter an adjacent garrisoned city of Wanping to conduct a search. When permission was refused by Chinese authorities, the Japanese suddently opened an attack on Wanping with infantry and artillery forces. When the Chinese garrison offered resistance in self-defense the Japanese at once resorted to large-scale operations against the Chinese troops in order, to quote their own words, "to punish the Chinese army" and to "uphold the Japanese military prestige."

From that moment on the Chinese local authorities made repeated efforts to effect a peaceful settlement with Japan and, though the responsibility did not rest with Chinese authorities, went out of their way to accept the Japanese demands for an apology, punishment of the officers involved in the conflict and guarantee against recurrence of similar incidents, the replacement of Chinese regular troops at designated points by the Peace Preservation Corps, and effective suppression of the so-called anti-Japanese and Communist organisations in Hopei Province.

Chinese ready for peaceful settlement

The Chinese Government itself repeatedly proposed simultaneous withdrawal of Chinese and Japanese troops. Seeing that Japan insisted upon the so-called non-interference on its part in the local settlement, it went so far in the interest of peace as to refrain from raising objections to its terms. But each concession and every act of forbearance on the part of the Chinese Government or the local authorities was taken by the Japanese military authorities as a sign of weakness and fear and was followed by sending more Japanese troops to Hopei Province for the purpose of pressing forward the plan of conquering North China.

The real object of the Japanese policy was disclosed when the Japanese Army, after large reinforcements had arrived, attacked and occupied not only Tientsin but also Peiping, the ancient capital and the leading cultural centre of China. No sooner had they effected their occupation of these two principal cities in North China than they extended their operations into southern Hopei and northward into Chahar Province. Fierce attacks were made on the strategic Nankow Pass and Kalgan, an important city north of the Great Wall. Today the Japanese troops in North China total more than 200,000 strong and are continuing their invasion southward, northward and westward into the interior.

Japanese attacked and occupied Peiping, Tientsin

In the hope of coercing the Chinese Government to submission, Japan has invaded Shanghai, the financial and economic centre of China, as she did in 1932 following her occupation of Manchuria. Here again, in order to have a pretext the Japanese naval authorities provoked an incident on August 9th. One Japanese naval officer and one Japanese seaman attempted to approach the Chinese military aerodrome in the suburb of Shanghai in spite of the Chinese warning. When

Invaded Shanghai

they were stopped by a Chinese guard, a clash took place in which the two Japanese and a member of the Chinese Peace Preservation Corps were killed.

While the Chinese local authorities immediately proposed a settlement through diplomatic channels, the Japanese Navy concentrated thirty warships in Shanghai within forty-eight hours and increased their naval forces by several thousand marines. On August 13th, four days after the incident, the Japanese naval forces, both ashore and afloat, using the International Settlemtnt as a base for operations, attacked the Chinese districts of Kiangwan and Chapei. In defense of her territory and independence China has been obliged, here as in North China, to resist force with force.

The incidents, which appeared to have been the immediate causes of the armed conflict in North China and in Shanghai, are referred to here only for the reason that they have been exploited by the Japanese as convenient pretexts for resorting to armed aggression against China. In both these places wher hostilities have been raging in the past weeks, the original incidents were provoked by the Japanese and have since been forgotten by them. If these had not taken place, others would have been created by them.

The important fact is that Japan has been pursuing a fixed program of territorial expansion on the Asiatic mainland, and consecrates the use of force as an instrument to achieve her policy. When the Japanese Army was attacking and occupying

Manchuria in 1931, the official spokesman of Japan sought to justify the action by claiming that these three Chinese provinces constituted Japan's life-line essential to her security. When the military occupation of this vast region was completed, Japanese military authorities deemed it necessary to seize Jehol in order to ensure the security of Manchuria. No sooner had they occupied Jehol than North China, Chahar and Suiyuan became the life-line of the Japanese Empire. In the name of assuring strategic and economic security for Japan, the Japanese Army has started a large scale military campaign on China in these regions for the obvious purpose of domination and conquest. The lust for territorial aggrandizement has been the real motive force behind all her military adventures.

Japan's purpose — domination and conquest

It has often been claimed that the pressure of over-population in Japan, increasing at the rate of 800,000 souls a year, has driven her to seek new territories as an outlet. This is, however, only a pretext put forward to enlist sympathy and confound public opinion abroad. Forty years of control of Formosa induced less than a quarter of a million of Japanese immigrants to settle there. Korea, thirty years after her conquest and annexation by Japan, has only 500,000 Japanese residents. For a quarter of a century Japan has been exercising a predominant influence in South Manchuria, and yet hardly 300,000 Japanese have chosen to live there, and a considerable part of this number is composed of the military forces, railway

Over-population argument refuted

111

guards, the employees of the South Manchuria Railway and the Japanese consular service. The truth is that the density of population per square mile in Japan is not as great as some countries in Europe, notably Belgium, nor does it equal the density of a Chinese Province like Hopei. And the Japanese people themselves, on account of the highly industrialized state of their own country, do not feel the necessity of leaving their homes and settling abroad.

The fact that Japan lacks raw materials within the borders of her Empire and depends upon supplies from abroad is certainly no justification for resorting to armed aggression against a peaceful neighbor. Besides, most of her needs are supplied not from China but principally from other **Raw materials** countries such as cotton from the United States, **argument** oil from America and the Netherland Indies, iron **refuted** from India and Malaya, wool from Australia, and wood-pulp from Canada and the Scandinavian countries. As to coal and soya beans of Manchuria, the former had already been under Japan's control and the latter had always been available to her in the open market before its occupation by her armed forces.

China, on her part, had on more than one occasion demonstrated her willingness and readiness to enter into economic co-operation with Japan, but the Chinese good intentions have always been frustrated by the Japanese policy of the mailed fist. It is Japan's preference to plunder at the point of the pistol to cordial co-operation between two free and equal partners which has destroyed the prospect of an economic understanding between the two countries.

There are not lacking in Japan liberal-minded statesmen who see clearly that the future of their country lies in peaceful collaboration with other nations, more particularly with her neighbors in Asia, but public opinion as well as the Press have been muzzled for a long time by the war clan. It is not unnatural that after several series of political assassinations, Japanese statesmen are terror-striken and no longer attempt to lift their voice and make it heard.

Japan is once more in the grip of the war party which revels in keeping the people in a fearful state of war psychosis in order to unsurp political power at home and achieve territorial conquest abroad. It exalts Might and recognises no Right except that which is backed by the sword; it consecrates force as the arbiter of the destiny of nations; it glorifies war as an instrument of empire-building. Its idea of peace in the Far East is the "Pax Japonica", and its conception of order, abject acceptance of Japanese domination.

Japan — in the grip of War Party

What will be the consequence and effect of this endless Japanese armed aggression in China? To answer this question, it is necessary to understand first the scope of Japan's Continental Policy. Let it be recalled that this policy aims not only at the political domination and conquest of China, but

Its Continental Policy

also at the elimination of foreign interests wherever the Japanese sword holds sway and the eventual expulsion of Europe and America from their territorial possessions in Asia.

Menace to European and American interest

This statement is not made here with a view to alarming you but it is borne out in public declarations of Japanese statesmen and in the secret documents in the Japanese archives. The experience of the Western nations in Formosa and Korea, and now in Manchuria and Jehol has given ample warning in the past. European and American interests are already feeling the menace from the occupation of Tientsin and Peiping by the Japanese Army. If Japan should succeed in her attempt to dominate Shanghai as well, the end of the vast financial and commercial interests there of Europe and America could be easily foreseen.

It is clear that China, in vigorously resisting Japanese armed aggression is not only trying to defend her own territory and sovereignty, but in effect also to safeguard the rights and interests of the foreign Powers within her borders. If China's efforts should fail for want of adequate support from this great institution dedicated to the cause of peace and security among nations or from those foreign Powers whose special as well as general interests in the circumstances are common with her own, then the menace of Japanese aggression will soon fall upon them and the burden of defence will have to be borne by themselves.

Today Japan still bemoans the fact that her

national resources are unequal to her appetite for conquest and handicap her ambition to be the warlord of Asia. If the day should come, which God forbid, when she would be able to lay her hands even on a great part of what China possesses in man-power and natural resources, then she would feel herself so much stronger as to challenge the treaty rights and territorial possessions of Europe and America in the South Seas and the Pacific as well as on the mainland of Asia. History bears testimony to the fact that the ambition for territorial conquests rises in proportion as the means to achieve it grow just as the human appetite for food increases as the power of digestion strengthens.

The effect of continued Japanese aggression, however, is not limited to the menace to the territorial integrity and political independence of China, nor to the injury to the material interests of a few foreign Powers. The moral and spiritual aspect of the situation is equally, if not more, significant. It is a challenge to law and order in international relations which have taken three centuries to establish for the common benefit of the community of nations. Such chaos, if prolonged for want of timely checks, will nullify all the past work and present efforts to organise peace and security, and throw the entire world into the pandomonium of a general conflagration with all its horrors of killing and destruction.

In the face of this extraordinary situation,

what should be done? Can international law and treaty obligations be always disregarded with impunity? Do we accept lawlessness as inevitable, and are we prepared to see it extend its tentacles unchecked to destroy peace and order in the world? It seems to me that something can be done if we ourselves still respect the treaties we have signed and the Covenant which we have solemnly declared to uphold.

For one thing this policy of continued armed aggression in flagrant violation of international law and treaty obligations should be clearly denounced. As our honorable President has alluded to in his brief but eloquent address, in the supremacy of law lies the sole escape from the anarchy of force. For another thing, the illegal blockade of the coast of China jeopardizing the established rights of navigation and commerce should be expressly repudiated. It is the thin end of the wedge against the time-honored principle of the freedom of the seas.

Illegal Blockade of the Chinese coast

Furthermore, I hope that the horrors of deliberate and indiscriminate bombing from the air by the Japanese warplanes of Chinese and foreign non-combatants in disregard of the sanctity of civilian life have not escaped your attention and that every voice will be lifted in this Assembly to condemn its practice. As the recent British note sent by Mr. Eden to the Japanese Government has given expression to a universal feeling in the civilised world, the practice is, to use the words of the note itself, "as illegal as it is inhuman," because it constitutes a failure "to draw that clear distinction between combatants and non-combatants in the conduct of hostilities which international law no less than the conscience of mankind has always enjoined".

It may be claimed that the times are difficult and that there are preoccupations in Europe where the situation is anything but reassuring. But the situation in Europe today is really not unconnected with the situation in the Far East. It is a natural consequence of the failure to enforce the obligations of the Covenant at the time of the Manchurian crisis before the League. Peace is indivisible; and its maintenance is of common interest to us all. As recently stated by the Secretary of State of the great Republic of the United States, "Any situation in which armed hostilities are in progress or threatened is a situation in which the rights and interests of all nations are or may be affected." Our own Covenant says: "Any war or threat of war, whether immediately affecting any of the members of the League or not, is hereby declared a matter of concern to the whole League." These statements are not mere academic assertions but are based upon the practical experience of great statesmen and diplomats. If the problem of the Far East created by the repeated Japanese aggression is satisfactorily solved by the application of the principles of the Covenant, it is bound to have a

Peace is indivisible

most salutary effect upon Europe and will pave the way for an equally satisfactory solution of its own problem.

The League of Nations embodies an ideal and represents an order of international life which must be made to prevail if nations are to feel a sense of security and the world is to be a livable place for all. It is the only priceless issue of the great ordeal of the world which took place twenty years ago, which engulfed so many million human souls, and which has entailed generations of suffering and a train of problems from which the world has not yet fully recovered.

Principle of collective security — only basis for peace

The principle of collective security, which underlies the Covenant and which we have all accepted, is beyond question the only logical and sound basis for any sytem of organised peace in the world. It is the same principle which has enabled every modern State to evolve peace and maintain order within its borders. International life, if it is to be blessed with peace and order, no less depends upon the full application of this principle.

I hope it will be generally realized that self-interest in the maintenance of peace as well as considerations of justice and the conscience of mankind, dictate that we should co-operate fully and sincerely to devise ways and means to check armed aggression and reduce lawlessness wherever they arise in the world, It is in the loyal and joint discharge of our obligations under the Covenant and other treaties to which we are parties that lies the hope of extinguishing the conflagration in the Far East and reinforcing the peace of the Pacific and Europe.

The rapid success of the Nyon Conference dealing with the Mediterranean problem, though limited in membership, is a striking example of what could be done where there was a will to co-operate.

In short, the Far Eastern situation, on account of its utmost gravity, calls for urgent action by the League. The Chinese Government has formally appealed to the Council, invoking articles 10, 11 and 17 of the Covenant. It is now for the Council to decide whether to proceed itself to consideration and action at once or to seize the Assembly of the question at the same time or to refer it first to the Advisory Committee on the Sino-Japanese conflict set up by the Assembly on February 24th, 1933.

APPENDIX II

Speech By His Excellency Dr. V. K. Wellington Koo
Before the Far East Advisory Committee,
September 27, 1937

Mr. President, I wish first of all to say that my Government welcomes the opportunity of being represented on this Committee and of taking part in its deliberations.

My primary purpose in speaking, however, is to outline to you for your consideration and action the principal issues raised by the renewed outburst of Japanese armed aggresssion against China and the steps which, in the view of my Government, should be taken to deal with it.

The grave character of the situation in the Far East and the facts relating to its immediate origin and subsequent development have been given in the statements of the Chinese Government and of the Chinese delegation communicated to the League for the information of this Committee as well as of Members of the League in general, and in the speech which I had the honour to make in the Assembly on September 16th last. These documents, I understand, have all been laid before you and officially communicated to you by the Secretary-General at the request of the President of the Council.

I shall not, therefore, take up your time by dwelling on details, but shall content myself with recalling to you the important issues involved in the situation — issues of momentous consequence to the safety, well-being and destiny of my country and of far-reaching effect upon the future of the League of Nations and the peace of the world in general.

Before taking up this point, however, permit me to draw your attention to the fact that in the fortnight since I spoke in the Assembly Japan has rushed more troops to China. Her army of invasion in my country has now reached a strength of 350,000 men. They have attacked and occupied more cities and towns in the North and penetrated further into the interior. In the Shanghai sector they have launched new offensives which, thanks to be bravery of the Chinese troops, have as signally failed as their former attacks. The Japanese Navy has accentuated its interference with foreign and Chinese shipping through its illegal blockade of China's entire coast. The Japanese Air Force has intensified its inhuman method of terrorization and mass murder on the civilian population notably in Nanking, Canton, Nanchang and Hankow. This method of aerial bombardment is so revolting to the conscience of mankind and repugnant to the principles and rules of international law and decency, and carries with it such ominous portents for the safety of innocent men, women and children in all countries in future

Japanese Army of Invasion Increased to 350,000 men

conflicts that I shall be obliged to deal with it more fully later in this statement.

Japan's armed invasion of China on land, on the sea and from the air is a clear case of aggression. Whatever incidents there were at the beginning, they were of Japanese creation in order to have an apparent pretext for their plan of territorial conquest. Even if the incidents had been free from Japanese instigation, they could not justify such a formidable invasion of the territory of a peace-loving neighbour. Given peaceful intentions on the part of Japan, every incident, however serious it might appear in character, could have been settled amicably and without disturbing the peace between the two countries. For China had from the very beginning proposed and insisted, in the case of the Hungjao Aerodrome incident in Shanghai just as in the case of the Lukouchiao incident in the North, to settle these questions through the normal diplomatic channels.

It is also a fact on record that even after Japan had concentrated 20,000 troops and 100 warplanes in the Peiping-Tientsin area, China, after failing to persuade Japan to accept a peaceful settlement, had appealed to the Governments of the Powers signatory to the Nine-Power Treaty of Washington and the Governments of the two other Powers having important interests in the Far East, Germany and the Soviet Union, announcing her readiness to settle her differences with Japan by any peaceful means known to international law or treaties. But Japan persisted in her policy of force and plunged forward once more to invade China, in her attempt to realize her fixed programme of conquest on the Asiatic mainland. Her action constitutes an aggression, pure and simple, against the territorial integrity and existing political independence of China, a Member of the League, and a challenge to the League of Nations whose Members underatke, under Article 10, "to respect and preserve as against external aggression the territorial integrity and existing political independence of all Members of the League." It also constitutes a violation of the peace of nations which, under Article 11, is a matter of concern to the whole League.

Japan's Real Intention — Subjugation of China

The real intention of Japan is obvious. It is the subjugation and conquest of China as an essential step to the fulfilment of her so-called sacred mission to dominate Asia, the Pacific, and eventually the world. It may prove to be a mere dream on her part, but it nevertheless constitutes a real menace to the peace and security of nations. The responsible leaders of the Japanese Government have repeatedly and publicly declared their desire to "punish China" for lack of "sincerity" and relying upon their mighty war machine to "beat China to her knees". Let me ask what sins has China committed to deserve "punishment" from Japan. Is it because she has rufused to kneel down on her own initiative and kiss the feet of Japan? What sincerity does Japan expect from

China? Is it that of taking orders from Tokyo and doing its bidding?

The Foreign Minister of Japan, in his reply to the invitation of this Committee, tries to disguise the Japanese wolf in the Lamb's coat by complaining that the Chinese Government makes opposition to Japan and anti-Japanese agitation the basis of its national policy and professing a desire that the Chinese Government should entertain other sentiments. But what other sentiments China should entertain towards Japan are not specified. I presume it is not meant that the Chinese Government should cherish nothing but friendship, love and even perhaps gratitude to Japan for her never-ending invasion of China's territory, for her ruthless slaughter of tens of thousands of innocent Chinese men, women and children, for her wanton destruction of hundreds of millions of dollars' worth of property, and for her tearing away from the Chinese body politic one province after another by the power of the mighty Japanese arms. Is it by such methods of devastation and spoliation that the Japanese Foreign Minister expects to establish "a harmonious co-operation between China and Japan"?

The declarations of responsible Japanese statesmen betray the existence of a war mania and the lust for conquest in Japan as clear as the actions of the Japanese armed forces in China constitute a most flagrant form of international aggression. This attitude and this policy must be

Japan's Policy In Violation of International Law, Treaty Obligations

denounced because they are in violation of the principles of international law and treaty obligations including, particularly, the Kellogg-Briand Pact of Paris and the Nine-Power Treaty of Washington to which Japan is still a party; because they are responsible for the hostilities in my country and the sufferings of the Chinese people; and because they menace the peace and security of other nations.

What should the League do? I know there are people who are devoted to the cause of peace but who, before answering this question, would like to ask what could the league do. While I realise that the experience of the League in the past years calls forth prudence and circumspection on our part, it does not follow that nothing could be done and therefore nothing should be attempted in the presence of a grave danger alike to the safety of a member State and the peace of the world.

If the League cannot defend right in the face of might, it can at least point out the wrong-doer to the world. If it cannot stop aggression, it can at least denounce it. If it cannot enforce international law and the principles of the Covenant, it can at least make it known that it has not abandoned them. If it cannot prevent the ruthless slaughter of innocent men, women and children and the wanton destruction of property by illegal and inhuman method of aerial bombardment, it can at least make clear where its own sentiments are, so as to reinforce the universal demand of the civilised

League must Denounce Aggression

world for its immediate abandonment.

In the moral and juridical fields there is nothing that prevents the League from discharging its obligations under the Covenant. On the contrary, in the interest of its own prestige and of the cause of peace, the safeguarding of which is the *raison d'être* of its own existence, there is every reason that, confronted with a grave situation such as the present one in the Far East, it should pronounce its condemnation of the flagrant violations of international law, treaty obligations, and the elementary principles of justice and humanity.

This is particularly true as regards the necessity of voicing its horror and indignation at the inhuman method of air bombing on cities and towns by the Japanese Air Force. The ruthlessness of the Japanese war aviation in China has evoked strong protests from the Governments of the principal Powers and called forth the condemnation of the whole civilised world. The Press in the leading capitals, regardless of its political complexion or its traditional policy on foreign questions, has lifted its voice in unison against it and been demanding of the peoples in their respective countries to denounce it, to take concrete action and cooperate in order to bring about its abandonment.

League Must Condemn Indiscriminate Aerial Warfare

It is to be noted, too, that the American Secretary of state, Mr. Cordell Hull, following a warning given by the Commander-in-Chief of the Japanese fleet at Shanghai of the intention of the

Japanese Air Force to bomb Nanking, the capital, out of existence, states that "the Government of the United States disapproves of this imperilling of its citizens and of all the other non-combatants in general, as well as the suggestion that its civil servants and citizens at present residing in Nanking should evacuate the region in which they continue legally their legitimate occupations," and that "the Government of the United States holds that any general bombardment of an extensive region in which a large civil population resides is unjustifiable and contrary to legal and humanitarian principles".

The Note of the British Government to the Japanese Government in regard to the attack on the British Ambassador in China by Japanese warplanes, states that "it is one of the oldest and best established rules of international law that direct and deliberate attacks on non-combatants are absolutely prohibited, whether inside or outside the area in which hostilities are taking place". It considers the practice of bombing non-combatants "as illegal as it is inhuman".

According to the Press, on the occasion of the recent bombing of Nanking and Canton by Japanese airmen, the British Government instructed its Ambassador at Tokyo to express to the Japanese Government "the horror and indignation felt in Great Britain at the deplorable loss of life among the civilian population".

Since the announcement of their sinister intention to resort to wholsale butchery of Chinese civilian population, Japanese warplanes have already made nine bombing raids on Nanking, five on Canton and extended their ruthless attacks to Soochow, Hankow, Nanchang, Tsinan, Hsuchow and a dozen other cities levying in the few days alone a toll of death of perhaps 10,000 innocent men, women and children. A number of non-military objectives, including the Central Institute of Hygiene and the Central Hospital in Nanking, have been damaged or destroyed by Japanese air raids.

Japan's persistent resort to this form of indiscriminate slaughter of non-combatants is a challenge to civilization. If it is left unheeded, there is no assurance that the dangerous precedent thus created will not be followed in future conflict in the Occident. It makes one shudder to think of the possibility of this horrible form of killing and devastation being inflicted upon the great capitals of Europe and America. If the challenge is not squarely faced, there is a probability that other cruel methods will be resorted to by the Japanese Army in its desperate attempt to break the determined resistance of the brave Chinese defenders. Already Japanese official news agencies have been preparing the world for their adoption as evidenced by their repeated accusation of the Chinese troops using asphyxiating gas, which is sheer fabrication and only betrays Japan's own sinister intention.

The League of Nations, under Articles 23 and

25 of the Covenant, has a humanitarian mission to perform. In the view of the Chinese delegation it cannot remain silent on this aspect of the Far Eastern situation any more than it can refrain from pronouncing itself on Japan's flagrant aggression against China's territorial integrity and political independence. The least it can do in regard to Japan's illegal and inhuman practice of bombing civilian population is to place its condemnation on record and recommend it to the Governments of the Member States to take all feasible measures, so that it may to some extent help to curtail her power of killing innocent non-combatants through aerial bombardments against the most elementary laws of decency and humanity as well as against all conventional rules of prohibition.

As regards concrete measures to discourage the continuance of general aggression on the one hand and encourage resistance to it on the other, the obligations of the Member States of the League under the Covenant are clear. The Chinese Government believes that in spite of our experience in the past, there are certain concrete and feasible measures which the League could recommend to the Governments of the Member States for this purpose, and that the question of what measures will be at once most effective and practicable in the present circumstances to aid China should be studied by the Committee without undue delay. We particularly ask that, within the limit of feasibility, the utmost measure of

Concrete, Feasible Measures Urged

encouragement and assistance be extended to China, the victim of flagrant aggression.

In conclusion, let me emphasize again that the situation in the Far East created by the Japanese armed invasion is very grave. It calls for urgent consideration and action by this Committee. Every new day means to China, without counting the loss of life on the field of hostilities, the killing of more hundreds, nay thousands, of innocent men and women whose eyes are turned on the civilized world and whose hopes are pinned upon this great institution dedicated to the principles of peace and humanity, praying that one and the other will hasten to do something to restrain the unbridled forces of aggression, to rescue them from indiscriminate slaughter and to mitigate their sufferings. In the name of humanity as well as in the interest of justice to my country and peace in the world, I earnestly hope that this Committee will not let the main issues be lost in a labyrinth of procedure but will act speedily as well as effectively.

Speech By His Excellency Dr. V. K. Wellington Koo
Broadcast to the
United States of America from Geneva,
September 26, 1937

I wish to speak to you this evening of the grave and painful situation in which renewed Japanese aggression has placed my country. Japan has sent to China in the past eleven weeks 350,000 troops, a fleet of over 100 warships, and several hundred warplanes to conquer China. With these mighty forces she has been attacking China on land, on the sea, and from the air. She has declared an illegal blockade of her entire coast, and been making air raids every day to terrorize the people. In defence of her territory and independence, my country has been obliged to resist, and is still resisting, this wanton aggression from Japan.

I shall not speak to you of the so-called incidents which might be considered as the immediate causes of the present crisis in the Far East. They are of no importance beyond the fact that they were provoked by the Japanese as convenient pretexts for starting hostilities against China on a large scale. Given peaceful intentions on the part of Japan, no dispute with China could not be amicably settled. Indeed, China repeatedly proposed to settle these incidents peaceably through the normal diplomatic channels. But with Japan dreaming of world domination and bent upon the immediate conquest of China, every incident was seized as a reason for starting armed aggression against China. If those incidents of Loukouchiao and Shanghai had not taken place, other pretexts would have been created by the Japanese military authorities for the execution of their sinister plan of territorial aggrandizement on a vast scale.

The one dominant purpose of the Japanese military party is to make Japan the warlord of Eastern Asia and the mistress of the Pacific. The achievement of this purpose is considered as an essential step to the eventual realization of Japan's so-called sacred mission to dominate the world. Force is their chosen instrument to carry out their policy. International law, treaty obligations, and humanitarian considerations which all peace-loving and civilized peoples desire to uphold, mean nothing to them.

It is this fact which explains their wanton and deliberate demolition of the universities and colleges, their attacks on Red Cross units and hospitals, and their ruthless bombing of open towns and cities, levying an appalling toll of death and destruction. The cries of the frightened women and children on the approach of Japanese bombing planes, the shrieks of mothers desperately searching for their babies, and the wailings of little boys and girls for their parents, produced no effect upon the invaders from the air. The horrors and brutalities of the indiscriminate bombing of the civilian population by the Japanese Air Force were as beyond our imagination as they were sickening to the hearts of all people who were the unwilling witnesses of the tragic scenes.

It was sheer ruthlessness which led the Commander-in-Chief of the Japanese naval forces to announce his plan to bomb Nanking, the capital, out of existence and to call upon even the diplomatic representatives of the foreign Powers to evacuate the city.

It is the same fact which has led the Japanese warlords and their civilian satellites to assert their desire "to beat China to her knees" and "to punish her" for the so-called lack of sincerity towards Japan. The truth is that Japan is waging a war of extermination against China.

Such lawlessness is unprecedented in modern history. It is actually directed against China but its effect is bound to be far–reaching. It gravely jeopardizes peace and order in the world and threatens civilization itself. Unless the problem is courageously faced and resolutely dealt with by all the peace-loving and law-abiding countries acting in concert, chaos and disorder will spread throughout the world; and the day will soon come when no great nation, however isolated it may be geographically and however hard it may hold itself aloof from the turmoil, will be able to enjoy the blessings of peace and prosperity.

The present situation in the Far East is very much like a case of one's neighbor's house on fire. Unless one helps to extinguish it in time, there is no telling that it will not spread and endanger one's own house.

**China's
Special Claim
to U.S.A.
Sympathy**

I feel that my country, in her hour of distress, has a special claim to the sympathy and help from the United States. The leaders of the Chinese revolution, which established the Chinese Republic, the first of its kind on the Continent of Asia, were fired with imagination by great American political thinkers, taught by the lofty-minded, self-denying American missionaries, and inspired by the example of the American democracy. Thousands of Chinese students have stuided in the United States and carried with them to China American ideas and ideals. Their profound desire has been to build up a united, strong, and prosperous China on the model of the great Republic across the Pacific. Many of them have become important members of the Central Government and been putting their ideas into practice.

In devoting themselves to the task of building up a new China, they have placed their confidence in the assurances given by the Nine-Power Treaty of Washington and paid less attention to the problem of arming China against external aggression. For the very first article of this treaty states that the contracting parties agree, among other things, to (1) "respect the sovereignty, the independence, and the territorial and administrative integrity of China", and (2) "provide the fullest and most unembarrassed opportunity to China to develop and maintain for herself an effective and stable Government".

Japan, in invading and occupying a large part of China's territory and thereby obliging her to stop the work of political reconstruction and economic development, has flagrantly violated the foregoing provisions of the treaty. It is a violation not only against China but also against the United States and the other countries who have signed it.

The traditional policy of the United States towards China has always been one of friendship and helpfulness. It was Anson Burlingame who negotiated with the United States for China the first treaty founded on the principles of equality and reciprocity. It was the illustrious Secretary of State, John Hay, who, at the time when the dismemberment of China was threatened, persuaded the other Powers having interests in China to adopt a policy of the open door and of the maintenance of her territorial and administrative integrity. It was President Wilson, the great American statesman, who by his timely intervention in concert with Great Britain prevented Japan's enslavement of China through the notorious Twenty-one Demands. Again it was the high statesmanship as well as the brilliant diplomacy of

U.S. Traditional Policy — Friendship

137

Charles Evans Hughes, as Secretary of State, which made possible the conclusion of the Nine-Power Treaty of Washington from which I have just quoted above.

These marks of friendship have been graven deep on the hearts of the Chinese people and made them to look upon the American people with gratitude and appreciation as their best friends in **Chinese** the world. It is this sentiment which makes every **Appreciation** Chinese feel that he can always talk to an American with an open heart and receive him with open arms.

China, confronted with ruthless invasion by a most cruel enemy, is fighting to-day for her very existence as an independent nation. Chinese troops have been resisting the never-ending Japanese aggression with courage and determination but with very limited means. Their ability to continue this resistance and their ultimate success depend upon an uninterrupted flow of supplies from abroad. Any obstacle or difficulty placed in the way of her purchasing and shipping arms and munitions of war in the United States or other countries will only handicap China and help Japan, which possesses a mighty navy and a big merchant fleet.

If China succeeds, she with her 3,000 years of history and culture, her deep-rooted hatred of war and love of peace, will be a powerful factor for tranquility and order not only in Eastern Asia but also in the vast region of the Pacific. The United

States, by its geographical position and in a view of its moral and material interests, cannot, I believe, be indifferent to the future of this vast region of the world. But if China should be conquered by the Japanese army or fall under Japanese domination, then her immense reservoir of man-power and vast natural resources will be made by them to feed Japan's gigantic war machine and increase her fighting power in order to threaten the peace of the Pacific and the well-being of the United States.

Japan — Threatening U.S. Well-being

It is true, to adopt a simile used by Professor Arnold J. Toynbee in his comment on the Far Eastern situation, that the Japanese tiger in making his long expected spring, has chosen now to leap the Yellow Sea and bury his claws in the flesh of China. But this fact connotes danger rather than consolation for the other countries of the Pacific Ocean who are as yet left untouched. For it is not so easy to set limits to a tiger's range once he has been permitted to break out of his cage. On the contrary, if he proves to be a man-eater, his appetite becomes insatiable when he has had his first taste of human blood.

The problem of statesmanship today is how to prevent and avert such a grave contingency. It is my humble opinion that one sure way of achieving this object is to help China to succeed in her resistance against aggression, to preserve her independence, and by friendly but firm intervention in concert with other peace-loving nations to make the forces of war and imperialism realize the isolation of their country in the world, the danger to its future well-being, and the necessity of an immediate change in their policy.

We of China do not wish the American people to fight for us, nor do we want to see the United States otherwise involved in the present conflict. China has all the fighting men she needs. Her **Moral Support,** soldiers have been resisting the invader bravely and **Material Aid** are determined to continue their resistance. But **Needed by China** she does need moral support and material aid in order to enable her to cope successfully with the present crisis — a success which is equally essential for her national existence and the cause of general peace.

I earnestly hope, therefore, that the American people will not desert their loyal friend, China, in her hour of distress, nor be indifferent to her fate, but will wholehartedly support her under the guidance of their great President, whose devotion and contribution to the cause of peace and friendly understanding between nations is already a by-word in every household, so that law and order may prevail in international relations and the peace of the Pacific be assured for the future.

APPENDIX IV

The Nine Power Treaty of Washington
February 6, 1922

The United States of America, Belgium, The British Empire, China, France, Italy, Japan, The Netherlands and Protugal:

Desiring to adopt a policy designed to stabilise conditions in the Far East, to safeguard the rights and interests of China, and to promote intercourse between China and the other Powers upon the basis of equality of opportunity:

Have resolved to conclude a treaty for that purpose . . .

Article I.

The Contracting Powers, other than China, agree:

(1) To respect the sovereignty, the independence, and the territorial and administrative integrity of China;

(2) To provide the fullest and most unembarrassed opportunity to China to develop and maintain for herself an effective and stable government;

(3) To use their influence for the purpose of effectually establishing and maintaining the principle of equal opportunity for the commerce and industry of all nations throughout the territory of China;

(4) To refrain from taking advantage of conditions in China in order to seek special rights or privileges which would abridge the rights of subjects or citizens of friendly States, and from countenancing action inimical to the security of such States.

Article II.

The Contracting Powers agree not to enter into any treaty, agreement, arrangement or understanding, either with one another, or, individually or collectively, with any Power or Powers, which would infringe or impair the principles stated in Article I.

Article III.

With a view to applying more effectually the principles of the Open Door or equality of opportunity in China for the trade and industry of all nations, the Contracting Powers, other than China, agree that they will not seek, nor support their respective nationals in seeking—

a) any arrangement which might pruport to establish in favour of their interests any general superiority of rights with respect to commercial or economic development in any designated region of China;

b) any such monopoly or preference as would deprive the nationals of any other Power of the right of undertaking any legitimate trade or industry in China, or of participating with the Chinese Government, or with any authority, in any category of public enterprise, or which by reason of its scope, duration or geographical extent is calculated to frustrate the practical application of the principle of equal opportunity.

It is understood that the foregoing stipulations of this Article are not to be so construed as to prohibit the acquisition of such properties or rights as may be necessary to the conduct of a particular commercial, industrial or financial undertaking or to the encouragement of invention and research.

China undertakes to be guided by the principles stated in the foregoing stipulations of this Article in dealing with applications for economic rights and privileges from Governments and nationals of all foreign countries, whether parties to the present Treaty or not.

Article IV.

The Contracting Powers agree not to support any aggreements by their respective nationals with each other designed to create Spheres of Influence or to provide for the enjoyment of mutually exclusive opportunities in designated parts of Chinese territory.

Article V.

China agrees that, throughout the whole of the railways in China, she will not exercise or permit unfair discrimination of any kind. In particular there shall be no discrimination whatever, direct or indirect, in respect of charges or of facilities on the ground of the nationality of passengers or the countries from which or to which they are proceeding, or the origin or ownership of goods or the country from which or to which they are consigned, or the nationality or ownership of the ship or other means of conveying such passengers or goods before or after their transport on the Chinese Railways.

The Contracting Powers, other then China, assume a corresponding obligation in respect of any of the aforesaid railways over which they or their nationals are in a position to exercise any control in virtue of any concession, special agreement or otherwise.

Article VI.

The Contracting Powers, other than China, agree fully to respect China's rights as a neutral in time of war to which China will observe the obligations of neutrality.

Article VII.

The Contracting Powers agree that, whenever a situation arises which in the opinion of any one of them involves the application of the stipulations of the present Treaty, and renders desirable discussion of such application, there shall be full and frank communication between the Contracting Powers concerned.

Article VIII.

Powers not signatory to the present Treaty, which have Governments recognized by the Signatory Powers and which have treaty relations with China, shall be invited to adhere to the present Treaty. To this end the Government of the United States will make the necessary communications to the non-signatory Powers and will inform the Contracting Powers of the replies received. Adherence by any Power shall become effective on receipt of notice thereof by the Government of the United States.

Article IX.

The present Treaty shall be ratified by the Contracting Powers in accordance with their respective constitutional methods and shall take effect on the date of the deposit of all the ratifications which shall take place at Washington as soon as possible. The Government of the United States will transmit to the other Contracting Powers a certified copy of the procès-verbal of the deposit of ratifications.

The present Treaty of which the French and English texts are both authentic, shall remain deposited in the archives of the Government of the United States, and duly certified copies thereof shall be transmitted by that Government to the other Contracting Powers.

In faith whereof the above-named Plenipotentiaries have signed the present Treaty.

Done at the City of Washington the Sixth day of February, One Thousand Nine Hundred and Twenty-Two.

APPENDIX V

The Report of the Brussels Conference,
November 24, 1937

1. The Conference at Brussels was assembled pursuant to an invitation extended by the Belgian Government at the request of His Majesty's Government in the United Kingdom with the approval of the American Government. It held its opening session on November 3, 1937. The Conference has now reached a point at which it appears desirable to record the essential phases of its work.

2. In the winter of 1921-22 there were signed at Washington a group of inter-related treaties and agreements of which the Nine Power Treaty regarding principles and policies to be followed in matters concerning China constituted one of the most important units. These treaties and agreements were the result of caeful deliberation and were entered upon freely. They were designed primarily to bring about conditions of stability and security in the Pacific area.

The Nine Power Treaty stipulated in Article I that "the Contracting Powers, other than China, agree:

(1) To respect the sovereignty, the independence, and the territorial and administrative integrity of China;

(2) To provide the fullest and most unembarrassed opportunity to China to develop and maintain for herself an effective and stable government;

(3) To use their influence for the purpose of effectually establishing and maintaining the principle of equal opportunity for the commerce and industry of all nations throughout the territory of China;

(4) To refrain from taking advantage of conditions in China in order to seek special rights or privileges which would abridge the rights of subjects or citizens of friendly States, and from countenancing action inimical to the security of such States."

Under and in the light of these undertakings and of the provisions contained in the other treaties, the situation in the Pacific area was for a decade characterized by a substantial measure of stability, with considerable progress toward the other objectives envisaged in the treaties. In recent years there have come a series of conflicts between Japan and China, and these conflicts have culminated in the hostilities now in progress.

3. The conference at Brussels was called for the purpose, as set forth in the terms of the invitation "of examining in accordance with Article VII of the Nine Power Treaty, the situation in the Far East and to consider friendly peaceable methods for hastening the end of the regrettable conflict now taking place there." With the exception of Japan, all of the signatories and adherents to the Nine Power Treaty of February 6, 1922 accepted the invitation and sent representatives to Brussels, for the purpose stated in the invitation.

4. The Chinese Government, attending the Conference and participating in its deliberations, has communicated with the other parties to the Nine Power Treaty in conformity with Article VII of that Treaty. It has stated here that its present military operations are purely in resistance to armed invasion of China by Japan. It has declared its willingness to accept a peace based upon the

principles of the Nine Power Treaty and to collaborate wholeheartedly with the other Powers in support of the principle of the sanctity of treaties.

5. The Japanese Government, in replying with regret that it was not able to accept the invitation to the Conference, affirmed that "the action of Japan in China is a measure of self-defense which she has been compelled to take in the face of China's fierce anti-Japanese policy and practice, and especially by her provocative action in resorting to force of arms; and consequently it lies, as has been declared already by the Imperial Government, outside the purview of the Nine Power Treaty"; and advanced the view that an attempt to seek a solution at a gathering of so many Powers "would only serve to complicate the situation still further and to put serious obstacles in the path of a just and proper solution."

6. On November 7, 1937, the Conference sent, through the Belgian Government, to the Japanese Government, a communication in the course of which the Conference inquired whether the Japanese Government would be willing to depute a representative or representatives to exchange views with representatives of a small number of Powers to be chosen for that purpose, the exchange of views to take place within the framework of the Nine Power Treaty and in conformity with the provisions of that treaty, toward throwing further light on points of difference and facilitating a settlement of the Sino-Japanese conflict. In that communication the representatives of the States met at Brussels expressed their earnest desire that peaceful settlement be achieved.

7. To that communication the Japanese Government replied in a communication of November 12, 1937, stating that it could not do otherwise than maintain its previously expressed point of view that the present action of Japan in her relations with China was a

measure of self-defense and did not come within the scope of the Nine Power Treaty; that only an effort between the two parties would constitute a means of securing the most just and the most equitable settlement, and that the intervention of a collective organ such as the Conference would merely excite public opinion in the two countries and make it more difficult to reach a solution satisfactory to all.

8. On November 15, the Conference adopted a declaration in the course of which it affirmed that the representatives of the Union of South Africa, the United States of America, Australia, Belgium, Bolivia, Canada, China, France, the United Kingdom, India, Mexico, Netherlands, New Zealand, Portugal and the Union of Socialist Soviet Republics " . . . consider that this conflict of concern in law to all countries party to the Nine Power Treaty of Washington of 1922 and to all countries party to the Pact of Paris of 1928 and of concern in fact to all countries members of the family of nations."

9. In the presence of this difference between the views of the Conference and of the Japanese Government there now appears to be no opportunity at this time for the Conference to carry out its terms of reference insofar as they relate to entering into discussions with Japan towards bringing about peace by agreement. The Conference therefore is concluding this phase of its work and at this moment of going into recess adopts a further declaration of its views.

10. The text of the communication sent to the Japanese Government on November 7th, 1937, reads as follows:

(1) The representatives of the States met in Brussels on November 3rd last have taken cognisance of the reply which the Japanese Government sent in on October 27th to the invitation of the Belgian Government, and the statement which accompanied

this reply.

(2) In these documents the Imperial Government states that it cherishes no territorial ambitions in respect of China and that on the contrary it sincerely desires "to assist in the material and moral development of the Chinese nation," that it also desires "to promote cultural and economic co-operation" with the foreign Powers in China and that it intends futhermore scrupulously "to respect foreign rights and interests in that country."

(3) The points referred to in this declaration are among the fundamental principles of the Treaty of Washington of February 6, 1922 (the Nine Power Treaty). The representatives of the States parties to this Treaty have taken note of the declarations of the Imperial Government in this respect.

(4) The Imperial Government moreover denies that there can be any question of a violation of the Nine Power Treaty by Japan and it formulates a number of complaints against the Chinese Government. The Chinese Government for its part contends that there has been violation, denies the charges of the Japanese Government and, in turn, makes complaint against Japan.

(5) The Treaty has made provision for just such a situation. It should be borne in mind that the exchange of views taking place in Brussels is based essentially on these provisions and constitutes "full and frank communication" as envisaged in Article VII. This Conference is being held with a view to assisting in the resolving by peaceful means of a conflict between parties to the Treaty.

One of the parties to the present conflict, China, is represented at the Conference and has affirmed its willingness fully to co-operate in its work.

The Conference regrets the absence of the other party,

Japan, whose co-operatin is most desirable.

(6) The Imperial Government states that it is "firmly convinced that an attempt to seek a solution at a gathering of so many Powers whose interests in East Asia are of varying degree, or who have practically no interests there at all, will only serve to complicate the situation still further and to put serious obstacles in the path of a just and proper solution."

It should be pointed out that all of these Powers which are parties to the Treaty are, under the terms of this instrument, entitled to exercise the rights which the Treaty confers upon them; that all Powers which have interests in the Far East are concerned regarding the present hostilities; and that the whole world is solicitous with regard to the effect of these hostilities on the peace and security of the members of the nations.

However, the representatives of the States met at Brussels believe tht it may be possible to allay Japan's misgivings referred to above; they would be glad to know whether the Imperial Government would be disposed to depute a representative or representatives to exchange views with representatives of a small number of Powers to be chosen for that purpose. Such an exchange of views would take place within the framework of the Nine Power Treaty and in conformity with the provisions of that Treaty. Its aims would be to throw further light on the various points referred to above and to facilitate a settlement of the conflict. Regretting the continuation of hostilities, being firmly convinced that a peaceful settlement is alone capable of ensuring a lasting and constructive solution of the present conflict, and having confidence in the efficacy of methods of conciliation, the representatives of the States met at Brussels earnestly desire that such a settlement may be achieved.

(7) The States represented at the Conference would be

very glad to know as soon as possible the attitude of the Imperial Government towards this proposal.

11. The text of the declaration adopted by the Conference on November 15, 1937, reads as follows:

The Representatives of the Union of South Africa, the United States of America, Australia, Belgium, Bolivia, Canada, China, France, The United Kingdom, India, Mexico, Netherlands, New Zealand, Portugal and the Union of Socialist Soviet Republics have drawn up the following declaration:

(1) The representatives of the above-mentioned States met at Brussels, having taken cognisance of the Japanese Government's reply of November 12, 1937, to the communication addressed to the latter on November 7, 1937, observe with regret that the Japanese Government still contends that the conflict between Japan and China lies outside the scope of the Nine Power Treaty and again declines to enter into an exchange of views for the purpose of endeavoring to achieve a peaceful settlement of that conflict.

(2) It is clear that the Japanese concept of the issues and interests involved in the conflict under reference is utterly different from the concept of most of the other nations and governments of the world. The Japanese Government insist that, as the conflict is between Japan and China, it concerns those two countries only. Against this, the representatives of the above-mentioned States now met at Brussels consider this conflict of concern in law to all countries party to the Nine Power Treaty of Washington of 1922 and to all countries party to the Pact of Paris of 1928, and of concern in fact to all countries members of the family of Nations.

(3) It cannot be denied that in the Nine Power Treaty the parties thereto affirmed it to be their desire to adopt a specified

policy designed to stabilize conditions in the Far East and agreed to apply certain specified principles in their relations with China and, in China, with one another; and that in the Pact of Paris the parties agreed that "the settlement or solution of all disputes or conflicts of whatever nature or of whatever origin they may be, which may arise among them, shall never be sought except by pacific means."

(4) It cannot be denied that the present hostilities between Japan and China adversely affect not only the rights of all nations but also the material interests of nearly all nations. These hostilities have brought to some nationals of third countries death, to many nationals of third countries great peril, to property of nationals of third countries widespread destruction, to international communications disruption, to international trade disturbance and loss, to the peoples of all nations a sense of horror and indignation, to all the world feelings of uncertainty and apprehension.

(5) The representatives of the above-mentioned States met at Brussels therefore regard these hostilities and the situation which they have brought about as matters inevitably of concern to the countries which they represent and—more—to the whole world. To them the problem appears not in terms simply of relations between two countries in the Far East but in terms of law, orderly processes, world security and world peace.

(6) The Japanese Government, has affirmed in its note of October 27th, to which it refers in its note of November 12th, that in employing armed force against China it was anxious to "make China renounce her present policy." The representatives of the above-mentioned States met at Brussels are moved to point out that there exists no warrant in law for the use of armed force by any country for the purpose of intervening in the internal

regime of another country and that general recognition of such a right would be a permanent cause of conflict.

(7) The Japanese Government contends that it should be left to Japan and China to proceed to a settlement by and between themselves alone. But, that a just and lasting settlement could be achieved by such a method cannot be believed. Japanese armed forces are present in enormous numbers on Chinese soil and have occupied large and important areas thereof. Japanese authorities have declared in substance that it is Japan's objective to destroy the will and the ability of China to resist the will and demands of Japan. The Japanese Government affirms that it is China whose actions and attitude are in contravention of the Nine Power Treaty; yet, whereas China is engaged in full and frank discussion of the matter with the other parties to that Treaty, Japan refuses to discuss it with any of them. Chinese authorities have repeatedly declared that they will not, in fact that they cannot, negotiate with Japan alone for a settlement by agreement. In these circumstances, there is no ground for any belief that, if left to themselves, Japan and China would arrive in the appreciably near future at any solution which would give promise of peace between those two countries, security for the rights and interests of other countries, and political and economic stability in the Far East. On the contrary, there is every reason to believe that if this matter were left entirely to Japan and China and the armed conflict—with attendant destruction of life and property, disorder, uncertainty, instability, suffering, enmity, hatred and disturbance to the whole world—would continue indefinitely.

(8) The Japanese Government, in their latest communication, invite the Powers represented at Brussels to make a contribution to the stability of Eastern Asia in accordance with the realities of the situation.

(9) In the view of the representatives of the above-mentioned States met at Brussels, the essential realities of the situation are those to which they draw attention above.

(10) The representatives of the above-mentioned States met at Brussels are firmly of the belief that, for the reasons given above, a just and durable settlement is not to be expected of direct negotiations between the parties. That is why, in the communications addressed to the Japanese Government, they invited that Government to confer with them or with representatives of a small number of Powers to be chosen for that purpose, in the hope that such exchange of views might lead to acceptance of their good offices and thus help towards the negotiation of a satisfactory settlement.

(11) They will believe that if the parties to the conflict would agree to a cessation of hostilities in order to give an opportunity for such a procedure to be tried, success might be achieved. The Chinese Delegation has intimated its readiness to fall in with this procedure. The representatives of the States met at Brussels find it difficult to understand Japan's persistent refusal to discuss such a method.

(12) Though hoping that Japan will not adhere to her refusal the above-mentioned States represented at Brussels must consider what is to be their common attitude in a situation where one party to an international treaty maintains against the views of all other parties that the action which it has taken does not come within the scope of that treaty and sets aside provisions of the treaty which the other parties hold to be operative in the circumstances.

The representatives of Sweden made the following statement:

"No one can regret more deeply than does the Swedish

Government the fact that the Conference's efforts at mediation have so far remained without result. Having to take note of this fact, my Government, which adheres to the principles of the declaration but which does not possess the same political interests in the Far East as certain other Powers, feels that it is its duty to abstain from voting for this text."

The representative of Norway made the following statement:

"The Norwegian Governmant accepted the invitation to this Conference in the desire thereby to contribute if possible to a settlement of the conflict in the Far East by peaceful mediation.

"Nobody deplores more than my Government that the efforts of the Conference towards such mediation have hitherto been fruitless.

"I am quite in accord with the principles underlying the declaration before us and the venture to express the hope that it may still prove possible to obtain through mediation a settlement on the basis of those principles.

"Referring, however, to my previous declaration made on the 13th instant, I find it proper to abstain from voting."

The representative of Denmark made the following statement:

"I should like to associate myself with the statements just made by my colleagues from Sweden and Norway. Also my country deplores that the efforts for mediation have hitherto not met with success, and I fully share the hope that through means of mediation it may still be possible to obtain some results. For similar reasons as those given by my Scandinavian colleagues, also I think it proper to abstain from voting on the text of this declaration, while fully in accord with the principles laid down therein."

The representative of Italy made the following statement:

"Italy considers the declaration before us as a door open not towards the settlement of the conflict, but rather towards the most serious complications.

"Italy does not intend to assume the responsibilities that might devolve therefrom, and she therefore expresses her definitely contrary vote, while reserving her attitude as regards all that concerns the subsequent phases of the dispute."

12. The text of the declaration adopted by the Conference on November 24, 1937, reads as follows:

(1) The Nine Power Treaty is a conspicuous example of numerous international instruments by which the nations of the world enunciate certain principles and accept certain self-denying rules in their conduct with each other solemnly undertaking to respect the sovereignty of other nations, to refrain from seeking political or economic domination of other nations, and to abstain from interference in their internal affairs.

(2) These international instruments constitute a framework within which international security and international peace are intended to be safeguarded without resort to arms and within which international friendships should subsist on the basis of mutual trust, goodwill, and beneficial trade and financial relations.

(3) It must be recognized that whenever armed force is employed in disregard of these principles the whole structure of international relations based upon the safeguards provided by treaties is disturbed. Nations are then compelled to seek security in ever-increasing armaments. There is created everywhere a feeling of uncertainty and insecurity. The validity of these principles cannot be destroyed by force, their universal applicability cannot be denied, and their indispensability to civilization and progress cannot be gainsaid.

(4) It was in accordance with these principles that this Conference was called in Brussels for the purpose, as set forth in the terms of the invitation issued by the Belgian Government, "of examining, in accordance with Article VII of the Nine Power Treaty, the situation in the Far East and to consider friendly methods for hastening the end of the regrettable conflict now taking place there."

(5) Since its opening session on November 3rd the Conference has continuously striven to promote conciliation and had endeavoured to secure the co-operation of the Japanese Government in the hope of arresting hostilities and bringing about a settlement.

(6) The Conference is convinced that force by itself can provide no just and lasting solution for disputes between nations. It continues to believe that it would be to the immediate and the ultimate interest of both parties to the present dispute to avail themselves of the assistance of others in an effort to bring hostilities to an early end as a necessary preliminary to the achievement of a general and lasting settlement. It further believes that a satisfactory settlement cannot be achieved by direct negotiation between the parties to the conflict alone, and that only by consultation with other Powers principally concerned can there be achieved an agreement the terms of which will be just, generally acceptable and likely to endure.

(7) This Conference strongly reaffirms the principles of the Nine Power Treaty as being among the basic principles which are essential to world peace and orderly progressive development of national and international life.

(8) The Conference believes that a prompt suspension of hostilities in the Far East would be in the best interests not only of China and Japan but of all nations. With each day's continuance

of the conflict the loss in lives and property increases and the ultimate solution of the conflict becomes more difficult.

(9) The Conference therefore strongly urges that hostilities be suspended and resort be had to peaceful processes.

(10) The Conference believes that no possible step to bring about by peaceful processes a just settlement of the conflict should be overlooked or omitted.

(11) In order to allow time for participating Governments to exchange views and further explore all peaceful methods by which a just settlement of the dispute may be attained consistently with the principles of the Nine Power Treaty, and in conformity with the objectives of that Treaty, the Conference deems it advisable temporarily to suspend its sittings. The conflict in the Far East remains, however, a matter of concern to all of the Powers assembled at Brussels — by virtue of commitments in the Nine Power Treaty or of special interest in the Far East — and especially to those most immediately and directly affected by conditions and events in the Far East. Those of them that are parties to the Nine Power Treaty have expressly adopted a policy designed to stabilize conditions in the Far East and, to that end, are bound by the provisions of that Treaty, outstanding among which are those of Articles I and VII.

(12) The Conference will be called together again whenever its Chairman or any two of its members shall have reported that they consider that its deliberations can be advantageously resumed.

Bibliographical Note

The sources of this work have already been cited in the footnotes and, for the sake of space, are not repeated here. The details of each reference, such as the name and place of the publisher, the edition and the year, as well as any abbreviation, are described at its first appearance. Among the official sources are the publications of international organizations and government agencies of China and other countries. Both official and unofficial collections of treaties and other documents have been frequently consulted.

Of the unofficial sources referred to in this work, the *Reminiscences of Wellington Koo* is the most important. Briefly explained in footnote one, it consists of eight volumes. Dr. Koo has presented the original copy and related materials to Columbia University with a view to making them available to interested scholars and others. In this Bibliographical Note, it will perhaps help readers understand the general contents of the *Reminiscences* by giving the essential substance of each volume.

Volume I (childhood and education, 1888-1912, in 143 pages) describes his birth, family background, elementary and classical education, graduation from St. John's College (Shanghai, 1904), one year at Cook Academy (Montour Falls, N.Y., 1904-1905), studies at Columbia University (1905-1912), recollections of the Sino-Japanese War (1894-1895) and the Reform Movement (1898), visit to Washington, D.C. at the invitation of China's special envoy T'ang Shao-i (January 1909), meeting with Sun Yat-sen (Fall 1909), completion of the Ph.D. degree at Columbia University (1912), invitation from President Yuan Shih-k'ai to be his English secretary (February 1912), and journey to Peking on the Trans-Siberian Railway.

Volume II (first decade as diplomat, 1912-1922, in 295 pages) is divided under four headings: (A) Peking in the early years of the Republic (1912-1916): his career in the Peking government as English secretary to both the President and the Prime Minister, Counselor of the Ministry of Foreign Affairs, Yuan Shih-k'ai's monarchical movement, frontier disputes and negotiations with Great Britain and Russia, and Japan's instrusions on Shantung and the Twenty-One Demands. (B) As Chinese Minister to the United States (1915-1919): the Chicago Loan of 1916, the United States and China's entrance into World War I, the Lansing-Ishii Notes (November 2, 1917), and preparations for the restoration of peace. (C) The Paris Peace Conference (1919): as Chinese delegate to present China's case before its Council of Ten (January 28, 1919), difficulties within the Chinese delegation, the arbitrary decision of its Council of Four to transfer former German rights in Shantung to Japan, and China's refusal to sign the Treaty of Versailles. (D) As Chinese Minister to Great Britain (1920-1922): the diplomatic mission in London, as Chinese delegate to the Washington Conference (1921-1922), the conclusion of the Nine-Power Treaty in Washington (February 6, 1922), and negotiations for the settlement of the Shantung problem with the Japanese delegation through the good offices and mediation of the United States and Great Britain (December 1, 1921 to February 4,

1922).

Volume III (government service in China, 1922-1932, in 365 pages) first relates his political activities in Peking as Foreign Minister, Finance Minister, and Prime Minister, China's civil war and the Military Government of Marshal Chang Tso-lin (June 1927-June 1928), Adolphe A. Joffe's mission to China, the Gold-Franc question, negotiations with the Soviet Union (1923-1924), Sino-British discussion of the rendition of the leased territory Weihaiwei, the termination of the Sino-Belgian Treaty of 1865, the Boxer indemnity refund and the China Foundation, the raid on the Russian Embassy in Peking (April 1927), and reflections on the failure of the democratic system of government in Peking. The latter part of this volume covers his sojourn abroad and recall to China for consultations, Marshal Chang Hsueh-liang's military clash with the Soviet forces on the Manchurian border (1929-1930), Japan's invasion of Manchuria (September 18, 1931), Nanking's policy and the League of Nations (September-November 1931), his appointment as Foreign Minister (November 28, 1931), popular reaction and the temporary resignation of Generalissimo Chiang Kai-shek, and his functions as China's Asessor to the Lytton Commission of Inquiry (1932).

Volume IV (mission to Paris, 1932-1941, in 935 pages of the first edited draft and 1,377 pages of the preliminary draft) deals with his mission in Paris as Chinese Minister to France, pleading China's case at the Council and the Assembly of the League of Nations (November 1932-May 1933), the Tangku truce and the shift in focus from sanctions against Japan to economic and technical aid to China (May-September 1933), the reaction abroad to the events in China (October-December 1933), diplomatic activities in France and Geneva, and his departure for China (June 1934). Dr. Koo came back to Paris as Chinese Ambassador to

France after the elevation of his mission in March 1936. Then he notes in this volume the worsening situation in Europe, the outbreak of the full-scale war between China and Japan (July 7, 1937), his role as China's chief delegate to the League of Nations urging collective measures against Japan and to the Brussels Conference (November 1937) invoking the Nine-Power Treaty of 1922, as well as diplomatic efforts to secure material assistance from friendly powers.

The pages in preliminary draft form of Volume IV analyze the aftermath of the Brussels Conference, the failure of a new appeal to the League of Nations in 1938 in view of the European crisis, the exploration of the possibilities of joint action by the Western Democracies and the Soviet Union, the outbreak of war in Europe and its impact on China, problems of Sino-French cooperation with particular emphasis on transit facilities through Indochina, the fall of Paris and the French surrender to Germany (May 18-June 23, 1940), Japanese advances in Indochina under Vichy France (June-August 1940), as well as reactions to the Franco-Japanese Agreement concerning Indochina (September 1940) and the Tripartite Pact concluded by Germany, Italy, and Japan.

Volume V (second mission to London, 1941-1946, in 900 pages) recounts the general objectives of his appointment as Chinese Ambassador to Great Britain, five major issues between the two countries (the British War Loan, the Burma Road, the Hongkong status, the problem of Indian independence, and the war strategy), the United States entrance into the war and its impact on the Far Eastern situation, his consultations in China and talks with Chinese leaders (October 1942-March 1943), the British Goodwill Mission to China (November-December 1942), the Sino-British Treaty for the relinquishment of extraterritorial jurisdiction in China (January 11, 1943), his sojourn in the United States (March-May 1943), talks with Madame Chiang Kai-shek regarding her proposed trip to England (in San Francisco, March 1943), visits with President Roosevelt and other American leaders in Washington, the abortive attempt to arrange a meeting between Madame Chiang and Prime Minister Churchill, T. V. Soong's interviews with Roosevelt and Churchill, the problem of Chinese seamen, his role as China's chief delegate to the Dumbarton Oaks Conference (August-October 1944), China's relations with the United States and the Soviet Union, various diplomatic activities in London, and as Chinese delegate to the San Francisco Conference for the Establishment of the United Nations (April-June 1945).

Volume VI (second mission to Washington, 1946-1950), in 1,929 pages) records his activities in Washington as Chinese Ambassador to the United States, the Marshall mission to China, the Truman Doctrine, the American reaction to China's request for a one billion dollar loan, the Wedemeyer mission to China (July-August 1947) and its repercussions, implementation of the China Aid Act (April-September 1948) Madame Chiang's visit to Washington (November-December 1948), the American attitude toward the uncertainties in China (January-August 1949), requests for renewed aid in the face of the White Paper (July-August 1949), the retreat of the Chinese Nationalist Government from the mainland to Taiwan, extension of the China Aid Act (December 9, 1949-February 15, 1950), United States aid and the Chinese Presidency February-March 1950), the question of recognition and China's appeal to the United Nations (September 1949-January 1950), difficulties at the United Nations (February-June 1950), and the status of American aid to China immediately prior to the outbreak of the Korean War.

Volume VII (second mission to Washington, 1950-1956, in 4,413 pages) gives an account of American initial ambiguities with regard to the status of Taiwan and its consequences (August 1950-February 1951), China's position at the United Nations, the Mutual Defense Assistance Program and American aid to China (April-July 1951), the Mao Pang-chu case and its bearing on American public opinion and the United States policy of aid to Nationalist China (September 1950), the Sino-Japanese peace settlement (September 1949-August 1952), the Korean armistice and its effect on Nationalist China, General Chiang Ching-kuo's visit to Washington (September-October 1953), consultations in Taiwan with Chinese leaders (July-August 1954), the conclusion of the Sino-American Mutual Defense Treaty of 1954, the crisis over the offshore islands in 1955, the Geneva talks and the representation issue at the United Nations, and his resignation and departure from Washington (May 1956).

Volume VIII (ten years as Judge and later Vice-President of the International Court of Justice, 1957-1967, in 79 pages) briefly narrates his nomination and election to the Court, the deliberation of cases, life at The Hague, relations of the Court with the Royal House, the diplomatic corps, and the Dutch community, visits of foreign dignitaries and personal friends and relatives, as well as his final decision to retire in 1967.

The above is only a summary of Dr. V.K. Wellington Koo's life and career as portrayed in his massive *Reminiscences.* It should also be noted that Dr. Koo's speeches, interviews, and many other papers are not all included in the eight volumes.

Index

INDEX

I

Illinois, University of (Urbana), 67
Indian independence, 60, 61
International Bank for Reconstruction and Development, 71
International Court of Justice, 11, 74, 98
International Monetary Fund, 72
Italy, 21, 28, 31, 32, 38, 39, 54
    war against Ethiopia, 18

J

Jordan, Sir John, 3
Japan
    postwar territorial domain, 49
    relations with
        China. *See* Japan's hostilities toward China
        Soviet Union, 38-39
            Treaty of Neutrality (1941), 43
        signatory to the Nine-Power Treaty (1922), 28
        war with Russia (1904-05), 66
        unconditional surrender, 85
Japan's hostilities toward China, 1-5, 13-14, 16, 19, 22, 30, 44, 83-84, 107-111, 122-124
    conduct of illegitimate warfare in China, 104-105, 116-117, 125-126
        bombing of Chinese civilian population, 25, 104-105, 127-130

Japan's conduct of illegitimate warfare in China *(cont.)*
    use of poison gas, 25
    creation of puppet regimes in China, 22
    German mediation, 31, 37-38
    League of Nations sanctions, 19, 22-23, 26, 118, 126-127
    Pressures on Chinese consulates, 22
    Twenty-one Demands, 3, 52, 85
    War, Sino-Japanese
        (1894-95), 2
        (1937-45), 1-2, 14, 18-19, 52, 54
Jehol, 39
Judd, Walter, 58

K

Karakhan, Leo M., 66, 86-87, 91
Kellogg-Briand Pact, 2
Kiating (Kiangsu province), 5
King, Wunsz, 25, 36
Koo, Mrs. Juliana, 1
Koo, V. K. Wellington
    achievements and devotion, 85
    advocator of "A.B.C. alliance", 62
    American compliments to, 73-74, 77, 78, 96
    Assessor to the Lytton Commission of Inquiry, 9
    birth, date and place of, 5
    British appreciation of, 97
    broadcast to U.S.A. from Geneva (9/26/1937), 133-140

About the Author

Dr. William L. (Ling) Tung is a scholar of Chinese background and Western training. A member of Phi Beta Kappa, he was, for several years, a research fellow at the University of Illinois and Yale University.

Dr. Tung has had a long career of public service and college teaching. Prior to his settling down in New York in 1950, he served in the Chinese government as a legislator, administrator, ambassador, and adviser. He took an active part in the promotion of local self-government in China, and was elected as President of the Municipal Council in Peiping (Peking) in 1933. As counselor of the Supreme National Defense Council during World War II, he was appointed to a Committee of Three to codify the administrative laws of China. He resigned from the Chinese government service in 1950, when he was Vice Minister of Foreign Affairs.

In China, he taught at the Northwestern University (Sian), Fuhtan University (Shanghai), and Hangchow University (then a part of the Joint Christian University in wartime Shanghai). Before he joined the faculty of Queens College of The City University of New York in 1962, he was Professor of International Law and Chairman of the Department of Political Science of St. John's University, New York.

In addition to his numerous publications in Chinese, Dr. Tung wrote several significant books in English on international law and organization, as well as on China's domestic and foreign affairs. The following are extracts of a few reviews of his recent works in scholarly journals:

The Political Institutions of Modern China (1964). Dr. Tung's book is "an excellent and comprehensive textbook on the subject." *(International Affairs,* London, April 1965.) "He [Tung] has combined political and legal history in a manner which gives substance to each and flavor to both." *(The American Journal of International Law,* Vol. 59, July 1965.) "In no other work known to this reviewer is there so comprehensive a combination of explanatory and connective narrative with presentation of texts of the evolved constitutional documents as is that which Professor Tung has achieved in this volume." *(World Affairs,* Vol. 127, October-December 1964.)

International Law in an Organizing World (1968). "Dr. Tung's text is a model of technical exposition of theory and comprehensive presentation of fact." *(The American Journal of International Law,* Vol. 63, January 1969.) "His [Tung's] book is a significant addition and meaningful contribution to the better understanding of modern international law." *(The American Political Science Review,* Vol. 65, June 1971). "A superb book, valuable to any college or university library." *(Choice,* September 1968.)

International Organization under the United Nations System (1969). "The information presented is, for a text, practically exhaustive." *(The American Journal of International Law,* Vol. 63, October 1969).

China and the Foreign Powers (1970). Tung's book is a "scholarly and convincing study, presented without bias or national prejudice." *(World Affairs,* Vol. 134, Fall 1971.) "Dr. Tung should be congratulated for his excellent work in this book, particularly for its lucidity, brevity, and systematic arrangement. It is even more admirable for a Chinese writer to maintain such fairness and objectivity as are displayed in his treatment of so many controversial problems." *(The American Political Science Review,* Vol. 66, March 1972.)

Revolutionary China: A Personal Account, 1926-1949. "The book provides what is undoubtedly an authentic and credibly objective picture of the inside workings of the Kuomintang." *Publisher's Weekly,* March 12, 1973.) "The book contains a wealth of information, giving names of persons and narrating incidents with meticulous detail. His account is marked by an uninhibited and often engaging candor." *(Pacific Affairs,* Vol. 47, Winter 1974-75.)

BOOKS PUBLISHED UNDER THE AUSPICES OF
THE CENTER OF ASIAN STUDIES

ASIA IN THE MODERN WORLD

1. The Chinese Revolution of 1911
   by C. T. Liang

2. China and the Paris Peace Conference, 1919
   by Wunsz King

3. China and the Washington Conference, 1921-1922
   by Wunsz King.

4. China and the Nine Power Conference at Brussels in 1937
   by Tsien Tai

5. China and the League of Nations
   by Wunsz King

6. The Sinister Face of the Mukden Incident
   by C. T. Liang
   The Mukden Incident was a turning point in Japanese and
   world history, It signified the beginning of Japan's fateful
   march toward World War II.

7. The Kuomintang: Selected Historical Documents, 1894-1969
   by Milton J. T. Shieh
   This work was prepared for the benefit of those who are
   interested in the history and development of the Kuomintang
   (Nationalist Party).

8. Foundations of the Chinese Revolution, 1905-1912
   by Ta-ling Lee
   This study by Professor Ta-ling Lee concerns the role played
   by the T'ung-meng Hui (Alliance Society) in the Chinese
   Revolution during the period from 1905 to 1912.

ASIAN TRANSLATION SERIES

The Tao Teh Ching/Lao Tzu
Trans. by John C. H. Wu; ed. by Paul K. T. Sih
Ancient Chinese Classic. A written expression of the religious philosophy of Taoism. Chinese-English texts.

The Hsiao Ching/Confucius
Trans. by Mary Lelia Makra, M.M.; ed. by Paul K. T. Sih
A philosophical dialogue between Confucius and his disciple, Tseng Tzu. Chinese-English texts.

The Platform Scripture
Trans. with an introduction by Professor Wing-tsit Chan
The Tun-huang manuscript with Chinese-English texts. This book is also suitable for study of the original Chinese text.

Vignettes from the Late Ch'ing: Bizarre Happenings Eyewitnessed over two Decades
Trans. by Shih Shun Liu. Published by The Chinese University of Hong Kong in cooperation with the Center of Asian Studies, St. John's University, New York.

ASIAN PHILOSOPHICAL SERIES

Wang Yang Ming
by Carsun Chang
The life and thought of the sixteenth century philosopher whose monistic idealism shaped the mysteries of the East.

Chinese Humanism and Christian Spirituality
Essays of John C. H. Wu; ed. by Paul K. T. Sih
This book explores an area of equal interest — the mutual interplay between Oriental and Occidental culture.

Mencius: The Man and his Ideas
by Albert Felix Verwilghen
A lucid study of life, philosophy, and ideas of Mencius (372-289 B.C.) whose system of thought forms a major element in Confucian tradition.

Contemporary Japanese Philosophical Thought
   by Gino K. Piovesana, S.J.
   A study of the development of philosophy in Japan since the Meiji Restoration up to the present time.

Eastern and Western Cultures: Confrontation or Conciliation
   by Chen Li-fu
   A compilation of four lectures on this subject.

From Confucius to Christ
   by Paul K. T. Sih.
   An account of the author's spiritual experience.

Why Confucius Has Been Reverenced as the Model Teacher of All Ages
   by Chen Li-fu.
   This book includes also a Chinese text suitable for bilingual studies.

The Center of Asian Studies of St. John's University

The Center of Asian Studies of St. John's University was established in 1959 to prepare graduate students for careers dealing with Asia, and to aid research and publication on the Asian world during the modern period. In 1973 an undergraduate program majoring in East Asia Studies was developed.

The Studies of the Center of Asian Studies were inaugurated in 1962 to bring to a wider public the results of significant new research on important issues and subjects relating to East Asia.